Innovative Management Skills

Teamwork

Also by Vincent Nolan in the Sphere
Innovative Management Skills series

Communication
Problem Solving

Vincent Nolan

Teamwork

Sphere Reference Books

To Sheelagh, with love

Sphere Books Limited, 27 Wrights Lane, London W8 5TZ
First published by Sphere Books Ltd 1987
Copyright © 1987 by Vincent Nolan

TRADE
MARK

Set in 9/11pt Univers

Printed and bound in Great Britain by
Collins, Glasgow

Contents

Acknowledgements

The material in these books is derived largely from my experience of using and teaching the Synectics body of knowledge over the last fifteen years. This knowledge is based on videotape recordings of people at work and identification, in microscopic detail, of the practices that correlate with successful performance, in different types of situation.

In one sense, therefore, I am indebted to all Synectics practitioners past and present, and the client groups with whom they have worked (200,000 people at the last count!). Certainly the 5,000 (at a guess) with whom I have worked personally over the last fifteen years have provided me with rich material and insights.

In particular I am grateful to George Prince, a founder of Synectics Inc. and current Chairman of the Synectics Corporation, for his unstinting encouragement and sharing of his own discoveries; also to Rick Harriman, President of Synectics Inc., and my co-directors in Synectics Ltd – John Alexander, Jason Snelling and Sandy Dunlop – for their support and understanding.

Three experienced independent consultants – Reg Hamilton, Terry Simons and Eddie Bows – responded generously to requests for help in their particular areas of expertise. I have tried to acknowledge their specific contributions in the relevant parts of the text, along with those of other individuals, whenever I have been able to remember who first made the point to me.

However, what I have written represents very much my personal view of the world and should not be read as an 'official' Synectics text. Everybody who encounters the Synectics body of knowledge takes from it what is useful to them – here I am presenting what has proved useful to me.

I am also grateful to Brough Girling, who as my agent guided me through the strange world of book publishing.

Finally I would like especially to thank Lynn Hobson, who has typed every word of all three books, with cheerful calm and composure, in addition to her normal duties – all at a time when she was coping with her new responsibilities as Manager of Operations Staff in Synectics Ltd. Next time, Lynn, I promise I will learn to use the word processor myself!

Vincent Nolan
September 1986

General Introduction to *Innovative Management Skills*

This series of books appears under the general title 'Innovative Management Skills'. This title has for me two distinct but related meanings: first, the skills required by a management which wants to have an innovative business; and second, management skills which are in themselves innovative to some degree, and which in some ways contradict received wisdom. The link between the two meanings is that to have an innovative business you need to manage in new ways. I meet many managers who want new things to happen, without being prepared to do anything new themselves!

The paradox of our time is that the need to be innovative has never been more widely recognized, as a condition of survival in a world of accelerating change, yet the norms and values which are honoured and rewarded in business are those appropriate to the efficient running of an established routine business! To be logical, analytical, orderly, decisive and aggressively singleminded are valuable qualities for dealing with one part of a manager's role – the efficient running of today's business. But innovating, and encouraging innovation by others, calls for quite different qualities, behaviour and values.

The successful manager of the future will require a much wider repertoire of skills than the manager of the past, together with the ability to select the appropriate skill for the situation to be dealt with. When it comes to innovation, 'many of the actions and attitudes essential if subordinates are to maintain an innovative posture are, for the manager, counter-intuitive and counter to conservative training. Counter, in fact, to many of the expectations transmitted by the boss'* (and the company culture).

There's no better place to start the process of innovation than your own behaviour as a manager. There's a great temptation, especially for the experienced 'successful' manager, to assume that the way we have experienced the world is the way the world has to be; and likewise that the methods we use and which have made us successful are necessarily the best methods available.

In the last quarter of a century, new information has become

*George Prince, Chairman of Synectics Corporation, January 1986.

available, particularly from research using videotape recordings of working situations, which demonstrates that conventionally accepted ways of working grossly underutilize the talents of people at work. The world does not have to be as we have experienced it; it can be very much better, more productive, more rewarding, more satisfying and more enjoyable.

But to take advantage of this opportunity may mean abandoning some cherished beliefs and established practices. It may mean experimenting with doing things in ways that you have not used before, when you cannot be sure that they will work any better than – or even as well as – your habitual methods. That's the essence of innovation – doing new things with the risk that they may not work as expected. If the business is to be innovative, the managers in it must be innovative in their own ways of working, and they must understand from personal experience the dynamics of the innovation process.

They need to be particularly aware of, and sympathetic towards, the *emotional* risks of doing new things, the risks of feeling foolish, getting it wrong, being criticized or ridiculed. They need to know how to protect the fragile self-esteem of the individual as he or she experiments and learns from new experiences. The manager who is also experimenting and learning is well placed to provide the necessary support and understanding to others.

Each book in the series stands alone and is complete in itself. There are, however, strong links between the three topics – problem solving, teamwork and communication – and skills in the three areas are mutually reinforcing.

— The experience of successfully solving problems together creates bonds which strengthen teamwork, through shared risks and shared achievement.

— Skill in developing a wide variety of alternative solutions allows teams to work on a win–win basis – no one needs to subordinate his or her interests to those of the team (except occasionally).

— Problem solving develops open-mindedness, and open minds communicate better than closed minds!

— Good-quality communications prevent misunderstandings and build trust within the team.

— Problem-solving experience demonstrates that we all see the world differently (as a result of our different life experiences) and this diversity is a source of richness in ideas, leading to a high level of tolerance and appreciation for diversity between team members.

— A good team environment encourages open and honest exchange of information and ideas, and the emotionally safe climate in which problem solving and innovation prosper.

In an innovative business, the quality of communication, problem solving and teamwork needs to be of an altogether higher order than in routine operations. Management is working under conditions of high uncertainty; creativity and ingenuity are needed both to create new initiatives and to respond to the unexpected. The anxiety inherent in handling uncertainty calls for the highest levels of interpersonal skills if the full talents of the people in the organization are to be released and directed towards shared objectives.

The aim of all three books is to provide insights and techniques which will help the innovative manager to achieve this exciting and demanding goal. I trust they will be of value to you.

Vincent Nolan
June 1986

1. Teams and teamwork

Introduction

If you look back over your working career, you will probably be able to identify some periods, two or three perhaps, that were outstandingly enjoyable and satisfying. Your colleagues were a pleasure to work with, the boss was a good guy (maybe *you* were the boss), there was excitement in the air, laughter too, and you were successful or on the way to a big success. The job, the people and the circumstances all seemed to come together in a mysterious, positive chemistry. Those were the days, that was a good time . . .

It would be nice always to have such good times. I cannot guarantee that you will ever do so, but I do believe that by working at the issues loosely labelled Teamwork, you can greatly increase your chances. My own experience, especially of the fifteen years I have spent building the business I started, has convinced me that success in business depends critically on the elusive teamwork factor. Trying to understand that chemistry, formulating explicit teamwork objectives and working continuously to achieve them, are probably the most important tasks in management.

The correlation between the quality of teamwork and business success is simply explained in the following model (introduced to me by John Philipp of Synectics Inc.):

— The individuals in the team have a fixed amount of potential energy.

— Each individual uses as much of his energy as is necessary to ensure his emotional 'survival', i.e. to avoid getting hurt and to lick his wounds or get revenge if he is hurt.

— The balance of his energy is available to devote to the task.

— The diagram shows how the energy available for the task increases dramatically as the improving team climate reduces the amount of energy the team members need to put into safeguarding their emotional well-being.

Success and the team climate

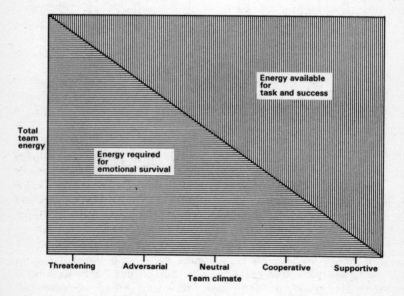

Although the model illustrates neatly how much the success of the operation depends on the quality of the teamwork, it tells us nothing about how to arrive at quality. That is the topic of this book, with the caveat that I do not have any sure-fire, cast-iron solutions. In fact, I do not believe there are any in this area; the appropriate level and style of teamwork depends on the situation in question, both the nature of the operation and the people involved.

Nor does the model say anything about the quantity of teambuilding activity required. This again depends on the people and the type of task they are engaged in. There is a strong temptation, especially among professional teambuilders, to assume that 'more is better'; an assumption which has been exposed and demolished very effectively by two of their members, Bill Critchley and David Casey.

In a perceptive paper called 'Second Thoughts on Teambuilding',* they argue that 'there is a very large proportion of most managers' work where teamwork is not needed (and to attempt to inculcate teamwork is dysfunctional). There is, at the same time, a very small proportion of their work where teamwork is absolutely vital (and to ignore teamworking skills is to invite disaster).' It is a salutary warning, and I return later (Chapter 2) to their method of distinguishing the two areas of work from each other and their proposals for handling them. The key issue at this stage is the need to be clear about the range of meanings involved in the apparently simple concepts of 'team' and 'teamwork' and the kinds of situations for which each of them is, or may be, appropriate.

The concept of 'team'

So, what is a team? I find myself wanting to resist this question, to brush it aside with a remark like, 'We all know what a team is; there's no need to be pedantic about it.' And I know myself well enough to be aware that that is a tactic for ducking the issue because it is a tricky one.

There is no choice but to attempt a definition and then see how it stands up. Here we go, then. For me:

A team is a group of people working together to achieve common objectives and willing to forgo individual autonomy to the extent necessary to achieve those objectives.

This is a pretty minimalist definition. It says nothing about the size of the group – the smallest team consists of two people only (as in the case of a husband and wife or a two-man bobsleigh team). There are even pyschologists who talk about teamwork between the sub-personalities within an individual person!

What about the upper limit? From sport, where much of the team metaphor comes from, we tend to think of a number like fifteen, from rugby union, as a maximum. American football, of course, takes us up to forty, albeit organized into specialized sub-teams and

*In *Management Education and Development*, vol. 15, pt 2, 1984.

substitutes. English football operates a 'squad' of perhaps sixteen to twenty, from which teams of eleven are drawn.

In the context of management, the old theories of span of control, which suggest that a manager cannot deal effectively with more than five to seven people reporting directly to him, tend to limit the typical management team to around seven or eight people. From my own experience of conducting participative meetings I know empirically that members of a group must not number more than eight if effective working is to be guaranteed.

Such conclusions point to a group needing to be fairly small in size to be considered a single team. Even a rugby team splits into a pack of eight and seven backs!

Does it, then, make sense to talk of a whole organization working as a team? (The Taylor Woodrow company has a logo of a tug-of-war team pulling on a rope and the slogan 'Teamwork builds'. The figures holding the rope always look to me as though they are about to collapse on their backsides for want of anything to pull against!)

I believe that a whole organization can work as a team if its members develop a common style of working that is constructive and co-operative and enables them readily and naturally to form temporary teams whenever they need to interact with each other. Perhaps this should be described as 'teamwork', and an organization viewed as a network of teams, temporary and permanent, following a common teamworking style, rather than a single large team.

'Working together to achieve common objectives' was the second component of my definition. In the sporting environment, the objectives are usually obvious; in the business they need to be articulated and made explicit. The functional objectives of a team are usually specific enough; for operational units they are determined by the organization's planning and budgeting processes, and for the staff departments by 'management by objectives' techniques or zero-based budgeting.

But a team may well have additional, less tangible objectives set for it either from above or from within. It may, for example, be expected to be a training ground which grooms people for jobs elsewhere in the organization, or to keep the organization at the leading edge of its particular field. On the other hand, a team itself may decide that one of its objectives is to create a high quality of working life for its members.

Whatever they are, objectives need to be not only explicit but also commonly understood. It is all too easy to state objectives and assume that everyone, inside the team and outside it, has the same understanding of them. I have argued elsewhere* that this is unlikely to be the case: the odds are not better than evens, and probably worse, that objectives will be understood the same way by all those concerned. Explicit paraphrasing and checking out is essential for something as fundamental as a team's objectives.

I also referred in my definition to 'common' objectives, implying that each member of a team shares its objectives and identifies wholeheartedly with them. In a sense, by joining a team, the individual member 'signs on' to that team's objectives; he enters into a contract as a condition of becoming a member of the team.

The degree of *commitment* with which he signs on, however, can vary enormously according to the circumstances. At the lowest level, he may be in the team because he needs a job, and this team was willing to take him on. He may have been compelled to join this particular team by the organization, as the price for continuing his career in it. He may have signed on with enthusiasm when he joined, but has now become disillusioned, or no longer accepts the way the objectives have changed over time.

In fact, the individual team member is in a team in order to satisfy his own personal needs, which are not identical with those of the team; in order to do this he is prepared to make a contribution to the achievement of the team's objectives. The better the balance between the individuals' contributions and the satisfaction of their needs, the more harmonious the team is likely to be. (I return to the question of the individual and the team later, in Chapter 2.)

The final component of my definition was 'willing to forgo personal autonomy to the extent necessary to achieve the common objectives'. By joining a team you limit your freedom to do as you like, but only, in my view, to the minimum degree needed for the team to succeed in what it is trying to do. If the constraints put on personal autonomy are perceived to be unnecessary, they are resented and commitment is reduced.

But the phrase 'to the extent necessary to achieve the common objectives' begs a lot of questions. What is the necessary extent, and can it be reduced in creative ways that allow the individual to maintain his autonomy without jeopardizing the common objectives? If not, should the objectives be changed? And at the end of the day, who decides?

Some companies explicitly demand that, as a condition of membership, the individual subordinates his own interests to those of the business. The philosophy of McKinsey and Co., the

*See *Communication*.

management consultants, can be summed up a follows: 'Client first, the firm [McKinsey] next, the individual last.'*

While it is possible to admire the quasi-religious fervour of such self-abnegation (and acknowledge McKinsey's undeniable commercial success), my personal ideal is rather different. I believe that the individual is in business for himself and responsible for his own decisions about his personal priorities in life.

I also believe that by using our creative abilities it is often possible to find a way to satisfy the requirements of both the individual and the team. There is usually more than one way of skinning any particular cat; if a proposed solution demands a trade-off between the interests of the individual and those of the team, it is not a particularly good one. Maybe, even probably, a better solution can be found if it is sought.

Not every situation can be resolved in this way, and how to deal with the trade-off is a matter of judgement. Ultimately that judgement is the responsibility of the team leader. (If a team is part of a larger organization, some of the constraints will be imposed by the rules and conventions of the organization. The team leader is then simply the channel through which the constraints are exercised).

Although the team leader has the ultimate responsibility for deciding the degree to which the autonomy of the team members is to be constrained, he has to exercise his responsibility in a way that does not erode the commitment of the team members. He needs to establish the constraints through a consultative process of problem-solving and negotiation, thereby producing an explicit set of general rules to be observed by all team members and individual 'contracts' covering each member's area of responsibility. I shall be returning to these issues, both from the point of view of the individual team member and that of the leader, in later chapters.

Team metaphors

Part of the difficulty in defining 'team' in the business context stems from the fact that it is a word drawn from the parlance of other worlds, particularly, although not exclusively, that of sport. In one respect, sport is a peculiarly inappropriate source of metaphor for business, because sport is ostensibly a win–lose activity, whereas business in the main, is a win–win activity.

This distinction is so crucial that it is worth some elaboration.

*Davis Maister, 'The One Firm Firm', *Sloan Management Review*.

Every sporting contest is designed to have one winner and one or more losers. In the language of game theory, sport is a zero-sum (or negative-sum) game in terms of the result of the contest.

Business, on the other hand, is about the creation of wealth. Although there is competition in business, it is possible for all competitors to be successful, in the sense of generating sufficient wealth to reward team members (employees and shareholders) adequately. Business is therefore a positive-sum game, in which it is possible for all players to be 'winners'. Competition may result in some being *relatively* more successful than others, but only in a minority of cases are there out and out losers, i.e. businesses which fail.

Sport becomes a positive-sum game if you take the Olympic or Corinthian view of it, according to which participation is what matters, the result being incidental. Timothy Gallwey expresses this eloquently:

> Winning is overcoming obstacles to reach a goal, but the value in winning is only as great as the value of the goal reached. Reaching the goal itself may not be as valuable as the experience that can come in making a supreme effort to overcome the obstacles involved.
>
> Competition then becomes an interesting device in which each player, by making his maximum effort to win, gives the other the opportunity he desires to reach new levels of self awareness.*

When using the team metaphor, therefore, it is important to be clear that, in principle, all business teams can be winning teams. Unlike a sporting team, a business team does not have to defeat its opposition to succeed. Its criteria of success are positive – the satisfaction of the needs of its 'customers' (in the widest sense of the term), who are the recipients of its output.

I think it is useful to get away from the sporting metaphor for a moment and look at some other types of team. They illustrate the wide variety of situations from which the team concept is drawn and may suggest diverse ways of thinking about the concept in the context of a business environment. (I am indebted to Terry Simons for much of the material that follows.)

Horses/mules/dogs

These non-human teams share a harness and pull together; the harness belongs to someone else – the driver! The team members just pull; all that is wanted from them is their muscle – no

*The Inner Game of Tennis, Random House, 1974.

intelligence, no individuality. The 'teamness' of a group like this is a measure of individual non-existence.

There have not been many direct human equivalents of this type of team since the time of the pyramids or the First World War – perhaps a Boat Race crew! In the business environment, I can think of the old card-punching rooms or groups of comptometer operators bashing away at purely mechanical tasks under the eagle eye of a dragon-like supervisor.

In today's business world, automation, computers and robotics should have made this type of team redundant, at least generally speaking. Of course, situations may well continue to arise that call temporarily for working in this highly disciplined and unquestioning manner – when it's 'All hands to the pumps!' to deal with a crisis, for example.

It's as well to acknowledge the validity of this mode of working in such situations, and to be prepared to switch into it when occasion demands.

The orchestra

An orchestra is made up of skilled professionals performing under the direction of a conductor. *What* they produce is laid down in the composer's score; *how* they produce it – with what nuances of interpretation (variations in light and shade, dynamics and the balance of forces) – is decided by the conductor. (As an amateur cellist who has recently joined a local orchestra, I find this team analogy particularly intriguing.)

I can think of many business equivalents, where the functional specialists are experts in their own field and the chief executive's role is to co-ordinate, balance and control (i.e. to be the conductor). In place of the composer's score is the business plan, its individual parts directed at separate functions and adding up, hopefully, to a harmonious whole.

Where the conductor and orchestra have an advantage over their business counterparts is in the instant feedback the one gives the other on the results of its efforts. Yet my conductor's repeated exhortations to the orchestra members to listen to each other would be equally apt addressed to members of a business team!

The conductor's ability to control is based on the respect of the players for his understanding of the music, his ability to communicate what he wants from them and his respect for their professionalism. Mutual respect is the basis of the relationship, with clear recognition from both parties as to the other's area of specialized expertise — not a bad model for a chief executive.

I am reminded of a BBC Master Class in which the conductor, Zubin Mehta, taught a cruel lesson to a group of aspirant conductors. He turned to the Israel Philharmonic Orchestra and asked them to start playing Stravinsky's *Rite of Spring* on their own, without his guidance; which they did quite adequately. 'That's what they can do without a conductor,' he said to his trainees. 'Anything you do has to be an improvement on that.' I sometimes wish I could set up a similar demonstration for chief executives!

The circus

A circus thrives on the range of talents that are exhibited, yet at the same time must have a degree of integration and coherence that makes it a single business unit that moves smoothly from one location to the next. You expect to see a lion-tamer, a clown, a trapeze artist, a juggler, a strong man, a horse-rider, etc., etc. (the more etceteras the better). Yet you expect to pay a reasonable amount for your ticket. You also expect the whole lot to appear and disappear overnight. In order for these expectations to be fulfilled, all the talents must be contained in comparatively few people, who must also play their part moving the big top.

This sort of team requires people who are not only specialists in skills that are unique to them, but who are also prepared to take on roles within the working unit in order to maintain the firm.

Most business teams have elements in common with a circus. Quite apart from individual skills to be exercised —

— juggling figures;
— taming customers;
— swinging deals;
— wrestling with unions;
— looking sexy;
— keeping everyone happy

— there are common tasks to be attended to:

— getting the best out of everyone;
— making things happen;
— seeing opportunities;
— maintaining standards;
— preserving external relations;
— obtaining resources;
— getting the product out.

Missionaries

In a team of missionaries, the members work alone. They go into the alien field to do their work, with very little interaction with other members of the team. They cannot rely upon the sort of support in their everyday work that members of other teams have. Yet they must support and be supported by the movement, by the cause. The 'teamness' of what they do is a sort of invisible net of confidence – confidence in each other and in the faith that they preach; knowing that, however difficult the opposition, they are contributing towards a whole.

This sort of team, typical of sales representatives for new products, speciality salesmen and political conspirators, needs a quite different sort of person from that required by a circus or Boat Race. Its members must share a bond of expectation. They must *expect* their colleagues to be playing an equal part. They must take it for granted that the rest of the team is preaching to the unenlightened – and preaching the same faith. This is why sophisticated bands of salesmen get together annually for simplistic acts of mutual worship of 'our product', 'our founder' and 'ourselves'. It is a means of reinforcing their expectations.

The lesson that emerges from this exploration of team metaphors is very simple; before building your team, you must be sure what sort of team you need! What you do to strengthen one could be anathema to another. There's no point in improving the autonomy of horses, going away for a religious thrash with a circus, or improving the working-together talents of people who hardly see each other for most of the year!

Before leaving the team metaphors that I think have relevance to business teams, I would like to examine a few others that in my view are not relevant and can be positively misleading. As well as looking at what a team is, we need to consider what it is not.

A business team is not a family. A family is linked by ties of blood, not common purpose. Membership of a family is involuntary – you are born into it; you do not choose to join it. The obligations of family members to one another go far beyond those of a working team and are based on emotion rather than function. There is a hierarchy in both the family and the business team, but the family hierarchy relies on parent–child relationships, not adult–adult relationships as does the business hierarchy. (For more about hierarchical relationships in a business team, see Chapter 2.)

Similarly, a business team is not a social club. A social club, like a business team, is motivated by a common purpose, but here it is the personal enjoyment of individual members, rather than the achievement of a common external objective. In a social club you can opt in or out to the extent that suits you individually, and still retain your membership as long as you pay your dues. A business would not survive very long run on that basis!

Finally, a business team is not a therapy group! A therapy group exists to provide an environment in which the participants can explore their emotional problems and discover new ways to relate to themselves and to the world at large. The bond between them comes from the mutual support they provide each other as they undergo similar experiences. Of course, a business team can benefit from an understanding of, and tolerance for, the emotional needs of its members, and a team of emotionally well-balanced people will probably perform better, over the long term, than a team of neurotics. (Although as I write this, I realize that it is more a statement of my own values than an observed fact. I can think of some successful business teams that could be described as pretty neurotic!)

It is also true that team members can and do derive satisfaction of some of their emotional needs from their membership of a business team – a sense of belonging and of shared achievement, for example. However, it is *not*, in my view, the responsibility of the team to satisfy the individual's emotional needs, rather the responsibility of the individual. He may well get help from fellow team members, but here they are acting out of friendship – albeit friendship that developed within the team – not out of responsibility as team members. I do not accept that the individual can reasonably complain if a team fails to satsify his emotional needs. That is not what teams are for.

Nobody, of course, explicitly claims that a team is a family, a social club or a therapy group – some people simply behave as though they think it should be! They impose unreasonable expectations on it, expectations that could only be imposed with propriety on a family, club or therapy group! Their disappointment when these unreasonable expectations are not met can be manifested in complaints about the poor quality of the teamwork. A sympathetic team leader can easily be seduced into trying to solve teamwork problems that do not actually exist – a dangerous diversion of energy.

McKinsey & Co. have an answer to this problem, too. They refuse to recruit people, however capable, whose ego needs are too great to be accommodated by their style of working!*

*Maister, op. cit.

Teamwork is . . .

Another way to try to capture what is meant by teamwork was suggested by my colleague, Lucy McCaffrey. Using the famous 'Love is . . .' cartoon as a model, she suggested we collected a list of 'Teamwork is . . .' sayings which might illustrate the variety of ways in which good teamwork manifests itself.

My own list was as follows:

— everyone pulling in the same direction;
— everyone pulling their weight;
— always having support available when you want it;
— being accepted for what you are, warts and all;
— going to do something you've overlooked, and finding it done for you;
— getting help when you need it and no interference when you don't;
— feeling it a pleasure to see your colleagues – at work and socially;
— everyone mucking in to retrieve a disaster;
— everyone pitching in without complaint when there's a crisis;
— enjoying each other's successes, commiserating with each other's setbacks;
— sharing success and failure;
— sharing an exciting vision of the future;
— being pleased to get together with your colleagues;
— depending on your colleagues to deliver what they promise;
— dancing to the same rhythm.

Various colleagues* contributed the following additions (exercising an editor's privilege I have selected the ones I like!):

— having people who understand to talk to;
— having people to help you build and grow;
— being able to sleep at night;
— not knowing who scored the goals;
— closing ranks against external, negative forces;
— enjoying working with others;
— being able to share when you want to (and not if you don't);

*My thanks to John Alexander, Jasmine Dale and Alison Cozens.

— a feeling of belonging;
— knowing what was said will be done (and if it isn't, hearing about it in time to do something about it);
— feeling of equal value;
— missing someone when he/she leaves;
— being able to enjoy everyone's good points, and live with their bad ones;
— not having to hold anything back — whatever is said is meant and taken constructively;
— a tree swaying in the wind — individual branches may break off, but the tree stays strong;
— knowing what your colleagues would think;
— sharing the load;
— the sum of the individuals' capabilities multiplied by the number of individuals;
— sometimes carrying, sometimes being carried;
— all working towards the same objective;
— a level of trust and openness which allows for total communication;
— knowing clearly who is doing what when;
— not having to be asked;
— knowing what you have to do and what you don't because someone else will;
— taking care of each other;
— looking out for each other.

No doubt you will find some of these resonating with you and others not; some may indeed conflict with your idea of teamwork. Maybe you can extend the list with some suggestions of your own.

Whatever else it shows, the list demonstrates that teamwork is a rich and complex concept, capable of many interpretations and meaning different things to different people. Later in this book (Chapters 2 and 3) I explore ways of giving effect to these diverse interpretations through the concept of 'autonomous teamwork' and interpersonal relationships of high quality.

2. Autonomous teamwork

The individual and the team

Teamwork, like motherhood and apple pie, tends to be regarded automatically as 'a good thing'. As with all good things, more tends to be seen as better (particularly by the 'experts' in the field!). To describe someone as 'a good teamworker' is a clearly positive endorsement. Describe someone as 'a loner', or even 'a bit of a loner', and there is unavoidably a negative implication to the message (unless you are proposing to parachute the person in question behind enemy lines!).

This pro-teamwork bias is, I believe, dangerous, because it tends to discount the importance of personal autonomy for the individual. People work with maximum commitment and energy when they are doing what they have chosen to do, and are doing it in the way they believe is best for them. If they have no emotional ownership of the task, if they are doing it only because they have been told to, or because it is merely a means of earning a living, they cannot bring their full energy and enthusiasm to it.

Clearly a business organization or team cannot consist of individuals all doing their own thing in their own way and in their own time. (Neither can a hippy commune – the experiments of the sixties revealed that here, too, people required some rules and shared commitments in order to survive at all.) Ideally methods of working are developed which integrate the cohesion and consistency of a good team with the personal autonomy the individual needs to work with full commitment.

I consider this to be an entirely practicable ideal and one which can be realized most of the time (though not 100 per cent of the time). As well as valuing their personal autonomy, people also like to work with others; they like to be helpful, to be supported and to identify with a whole (preferably successful) that is larger than themselves. It is natural, therefore, for people to work in a team, especially if it operates in a way that values and encourages individual autonomy.

The Synectics concept of 'autonomous teamwork' provides the mechanisms for reconciling these apparently contradictory forces. It starts from a recognition that each individual is in business for himself, i.e. to achieve his own personal goals and fulfil his own ambitions while continuing to live his life as he wishes, and that it is entirely right and proper that he should be so.

The individual has to achieve most of his objectives through inter-action with other people, who are also in business for themselves. In their interaction, they become a temporary team, with both parties committed to securing outcomes that are successful for both of them. It is a win–win concept of teamwork, just the opposite of the concept inherent in the sporting metaphors so often applied to business teamwork, according to which, for one team to win another must lose. It is a concept of 'mutuality of benefit', that is so well expressed by Mars Inc. as one of the five principles on which it operates:

A mutual benefit is a shared benefit; a shared benefit is a lasting benefit.

To secure win–win outcomes requires the belief that it is indeed possible to do so, and a degree of skill and imagination in problem-solving sufficient for the invention of numerous alternative methods of achieving the same objective. They are most easily secured when all parties possess these qualities, but they are still attainable when only one possesses them.

The underlying belief is that there is nearly always more than one way of skinning the cat; if the method I first think of conflicts in some way with your interests, we can invent an alternative method that does not, and/or invent other ways to look after your interests. The problem-solving skills required to do this are described in detail in the companion volume to this book, *Problem Solving*.

Synectics brings a whole new dimension to the concept of 'team'. My team now becomes 'anyone with whom I am currently interacting', including my colleagues in the unit, department or project group to which I belong (my permanent team), as well as outsiders – customers, suppliers, public authorities, etc. I am a member of one permanent team and many temporary teams, and the same win–win style of working extends to all of them.

It can even extend to my business competitor as well. We have common interests in expanding our shared market, maintaining high quality standards and finding specialized segments for ourselves where we do not come into head-on collision. In principle, I believe it should extend to the VAT inspector and the Inland Revenue, but I have some difficulty stretching it quite that far!

Clearly there have to be some exceptions to the win–win generality. Some situations are designed for only one winner – election to Parliament, for example, or a law court, where either prosecution or defence has to win. Some business situations are of this kind – airlines competing for a licence to fly a particular route, for instance. But business in general is about the creation of wealth, and if we are ingenious enough, we should be able to devise solutions that satisfy all the parties involved.

I am not talking here about compromise. In sporting terms, a compromise is a drawn game or a dead heat. Both parties gain something, but both also give up something and have to settle for second best. A win–win outcome entails both parties being positively pleased with the result, because enough additional value has been created to satisfy both their requirements.

Within the permanent team, the win–win style of working makes for maximum autonomy and mutual co-operation, and should harness the full commitment and involvement of all the team members. Again, there are inevitably occasions when no win–win solution can be invented and it is necessary to accept a compromise. If there is only one cake and no time or materials to bake any more, we can decide to split it or toss for it.

If a team member finds that he is *frequently* failing to satisfy his needs and resorting to compromise, it calls into question whether he actually belongs within the particular team. Every permanent team operates within its own norms and according to its own values, implicit or explicit; in joining a team, the individual enters into a contract (usually implicit) to operate accordingly himself. Difficulty in 'fitting-in' is usually a symptom that the contract has not been accepted or understood – not surprisingly, because it is rarely made explicit.

Because such problems occur quite frequently, there is a strong case for trying to make the norms and values explicit. In my experience, it is a difficult, time-consuming task to draft a concise set of principles which convey fundamental beliefs and act as guidelines for the way team members are expected to operate. It is also an extremely rewarding exercise, because it raises important issues and forces a team to think through where it stands in relation to them. As General Eisenhower said, 'Plans are useless, planning is essential.' i.e. the process of getting there is more important than the end result.

For the top management team of any organization, the articulation of the organization's values is an important part of its responsibility for strategic planning. Just as a mission statement summarizes in a sentence the unique purpose of a particular business, so a statement of values (or principles or beliefs) defines the character of the organization it is seeking to create.

To be of value, such a statement has to be genuine; the top management must themselves believe in it, and be seen to operate in accordance with it. (I know of one company where the statement is known as the Hypocritic Oath! Clearly, if it generates such a cynical response, it is doing more harm than good.) The values stated must also be promulgated actively throughout the organization and communicated in such a way that everyone knows what they mean in practice. Booklets, videos, training sessions and so on have to be used to ensure the necessary level of understanding and commitment.

From experience of working with two American companies that have put a great deal of effort into the formulation and communication of their values statements, I am convinced that they make an important contribution to the quality of management and teamwork (which is exceptionally high in both cases). I was curious to know how widespread the practice was in UK industry, so I wrote to the chairman of the hundred largest companies to ask for their company's equivalent statement.

The response was illuminating. Not more than a dozen companies replied, and only one or two had anything of the kind I was looking for. Interestingly, two of the largest, which were both going through a period of major change, said they were currently working on it. Another chairman said robustly that he wanted nothing to do with such new-fangled American nonsense. All in all, an interesting dog that did not bark, and an interesting reflection of the quality of top management in the UK.

In the absence of any such guidance from the corporate level, it is unrealistic to expect individual departmental or unit teams to fill the vacuum themselves. They have to operate within the corporate culture, which exists even though its values may not be made explicit. But team members are well advised to discuss among themselves periodically what kinds of behaviour they wish to promote in their team (and also what to discourage!). A team functions better if all its members work to the same ground rules.

The existence of such understanding makes it easier to cope with the problems of the dissident team member. It helps to reveal whether he has specific difficulties which are susceptible to win–win problem-solving, or whether he is fundamentally out of sympathy with the team and its values and has never genuinely 'signed-on' and entered into the team contract.

If he is out of sympathy with the rest of the team, the sooner he and the team part company the better for everyone concerned. Trying to accommodate the dissident member can be an enormous drain on the team's emotional energy. In two cases in my own experience, both the dissident individual and the team prospered markedly after the former's departure (in one case the reduced team doubled its productivity).

There is a psychological theory that every team has to have a scapegoat. The dissident member is merely the focus of unresolved conflicts and dissatisfaction in the team as a whole. It is an intellectually intriguing theory (and one that seems to appeal to intriguing intellectuals!). I do not know what empirical evidence there is for it; my own experience is that we have problem members at some times and not at others, but I am not sure whether we are more successful with or without them. Certainly the quality of my work life is much better without them!

The concept of action responsibility

For 'autonomous teamwork' to be effective, there has to be clarity in the team about each individual's roles and responsibilities. If the individual is 'in business for himself', we need to know *what* business he is in. And the sum of the individual businesses must add up to the total task of the team.

The concept of action responsibility is of each person being uniquely responsible for what he himself does, and not responsible in the same way for what other people do. Of course a manager is accountable for the performance of the whole organization he manages, but he exercises that responsibility only through the things he does personally.

It is a salutary, difficult and worthwhile exercise to describe your own action responsibility. It requires honest and accurate answers to the question, 'What do you do at work?' The answers must be specific and expressed using action verbs which describe what you actually *do* (preferably in language that makes sense to a ten-year-old child). The fudging verbs of the conventional job description – to ensure this, to control that, to manage the other – simply will not do. You need to explain *how*, to say what you *do* in order to ensure, control and manage these things.

For a senior manager especially, the exercise can have some alarming implications. First, not much that he does has any direct bearing on the success of the enterprise – he does not make anything, design anything or sell anything. Second, in doing the kinds of things that he does – specifying tasks, allocating resources, monitoring performance – he does not seem to exercise much power.

True, he has the power to award brownie points, recommend (or not) for promotion, hire and maybe ultimately fire. But this kind of power is pretty indiscriminate, rather like a nuclear deterrent – most effective when it is not actually used but kept in the background as a potential bribe or threat. The power to do the things that actually make the organization prosper (or not) – to design, make, buy and sell – exists lower down the organization (like the knives and handguns of guerillas in the jungle).

Your action responsibility defines your true power, the extent to which you can actually make things happen. It defines the space within which you exercise your autonomy; it must not be encroached upon by other team members, any more than you can encroach on theirs without risk of eroding their autonomy.

To ensure that each individual's autonomy is respected, the team can adopt what I call the 'mind your own business' principle, i.e. team members are left to carry out their own job in their own way, without advice, help, ideas, criticism or opinions from their colleagues, unless they ask for such, except when what they are doing or proposing to do impacts on another team member's area of responsibility.

Given the nature of most teams' operations, such interactions are likely to be quite frequent; they call for consultation and, if the impact is negative, some creative problem-solving between the two parties. The purpose of the problem-solving is to find an alternative way to achieve the objective of the proposed course of action, and/or to find ways to eliminate or deal with the negative effects of the proposed action.

In the course of this problem-solving, each party makes his own judgements about ideas that he would have to implement and does not attempt to interfere with his colleagues' right to do the same. So selling, persuading, advising and giving second opinions (If I were you, I would . . .') are out of order. For difficult problems, it is useful to enlist the help of a third team member, both as a source of independent ideas and to ensure that the disciplines are adhered to.

Solving problems together is a bonding experience that strengthens the links within a team through the sharing of the experience of success, and through the appreciation of colleagues' contributions. In a healthy team, it is not restricted to those situations in which one member's proposed action causes problems for a colleague. It is normal for any individual to ask for help whenever he is stuck or wants a better way to handle a situation than he can think of on his own. The initiative for problem-solving, however, must come from the problem-owner for it to be genuinely helpful.

Too often, enthusiastic team members, in their eagerness to be helpful and supportive, insist on imposing their ideas and opinions on colleagues who are perfectly satisfied with the way things are already. This not only wastes a lot of time (particularly if the recipient feels a need to respond politely); it is also destructive – the recipient experiences interference rather than help. Unsolicited ideas are easily taken as criticism. The 'mind your own business' rule is:

Offer ideas and opinions only when they are wanted.

This self-denying ordinance is not easy to follow. When we have what we think is a good idea, we feel it important to share it with the beneficiary at the earliest opportunity, regardless of whether he is interested or not. My colleague, Jason Snelling, solved this problem by instituting the unsolicited idea contract: when an unsolicited idea is offered, the recipient is under no obligation to acknowledge or comment upon it. (In a problem-solving meeting, he has strict obligations to check his understanding of the idea and to evaluate it constructively.)

Another difficulty is the urge to advise or help a colleague when he is not looking for advice or help. Clearly there are occasions when a colleague has a better judgement of the outcome of what I am proposing to do than I have (and vice versa), either from superior information, past experience or just a different perspective. In these cases I am foolish not to listen to what he has to say and to reconsider my decision in the light of it.

The way in which advice is offered is all important. If a colleague tells me that what I am doing is wrong and that I ought to do it differently, I am likely to resent his interference and to defend my actions. The exchange achieves nothing and damages our relationship to some degree. An offer of help needs to be extended in such a manner that it is clear my autonomy is respected. If a colleague says, 'I can see some problems that you may not have anticipated. Do you want to hear about them?', he alerts me to the dangers he perceives while acknowledging that I may already have thought about them. The choice of whether to discuss them or not is left to me. I cannot possibly object, and I perceive the offer as a genuinely helpful one.

The teamwork of the autonomous

The concept of action responsibility and the 'mind your own business', rule might seem at first sight like a denial of teamwork and a recipe for individualism. They are not, but I have given them emphasis to counteract a widespread tendency to subordinate the interests of the individual to the presumed interests of the team. Having stressed the autonomy, I now need to underline the teamwork dimensions of 'autonomous teamwork'.

There are at least four:

— the individual seeking help with a problem;
— interactive problem-solving to resolve conflicts;
— discussion of general team objectives, strategies and values;
— day-to-day supportive behaviour at the emotional level.

For the individual team member to seek help with a problem is not as easy as it sounds. The ethos of many organizations states, implicitly if not explicitly, 'You are paid to solve your own problems.' Consequently, 'to seek assistance is considered a confession of inadequacy'.* In such an environment, any problems an individual has are put down by that person to the shortcomings of someone else — 'I am certainly not going to confess my own inadequacy!'.

Team members who behave like this spend a lot of time and energy offering unsolicited ideas and advice to each other, criticizing each other (or worse still complaining about each other to other team members or to outsiders) and endlessly debating the rights and wrongs of their opinions. Needless to say, they never actually get round to *doing* anything to improve the situation.

I remember running a five-day training course for one group of

*Dr R. C. Parker, 'Creativity: a case history', *Engineering*, February 1975.

this kind in a major British company some years ago — and a difficult course it was. Towards the end of the fourth day my most vigorous critic said, 'Of course, we all do each other's job here', and immediately became my most vigorous supporter! He had put his finger on a key weakness not just of the team but of the whole company. Interestingly, he left the company not long afterwards, and it continued to progress towards its inevitable extinction a few years later.

Adopting the principles inherent in the concepts of action responsibility and minding your own business is a valuable first step in changing a situation of this kind: at least it cuts down the amount of 'noise' — purposeless and fruitless discussion. It needs to be reinforced by positive encouragement, so that seeking assistance is seen as a demonstration of open-mindedness and willingness to learn, rather than a confession of inadequacy. Someone seeking assistance will still feel he is running a risk by doing so, because he may indeed expose his ignorance of solutions that are known to other people. It is far better that he should learn of these, however, in a supportive environment, rather than feel the need to cover up his ignorance.

The problem-solving orientation of a team is reinforced by the interactive problem-solving employed to resolve conflicts (described earlier). Opportunities are signalled by any kind of argument or debate. (As a generalization, I would risk saying that if an argument cannot be converted into problem-solving it is not worth continuing!) A key question is, 'In what way is it [the issue you are raising] a problem for you, in your area of action responsibility?' If there is no satisfactory answer to this question, the issue is probably not worth discussing.

The one exception I would concede is when the issue is of critical importance to the success of the team as a whole, which brings in the third dimension of teamwork mentioned — discussion of team objectives, strategies and values.

Depending on the nature of its operation, a team needs to meet periodically — monthly, quarterly or at least annually — to clarify what it is trying to achieve and what kind of team it wants to be, and also to review its progress. These meetings are of critical importance to the success of a team (particularly if they are infrequent — frequent meetings provide more opportunity to recover from any that might be unsuccessful).

At their best, team meetings provide an opportunity to renew the cohesion of a team, to clarify the direction it is taking, to recharge emotional batteries, to sort out internal problems and generally to put the team on a sound footing for the forthcoming period of time. Conscious of this potential, team members come to meetings with high expectations and are disappointed if reality does not live up to these expectations.

At their worst, team meetings provide an opportunity for frustrations to be unloaded, smouldering resentments to erupt, unexpected problems to surface and sharp divisions to emerge. Team members rightly expect to be able to let their hair down and speak freely. The team leader has to be able to let this happen without it becoming destructive, a responsibility shared by the team members.

For all these reasons, team meetings present, in my experience, one of the most difficult areas of team management, and call for particular care and skill in their planning and conduct. It helps to start by acknowledging their importance and their complexity and by demanding that all team members share the responsibility for their success (though the ultimate responsibility in this as in all aspects of a team's operations rests with the team leadership).

Given their importance, dates should be fixed well in advance and in an ideal world are regarded as sacrosanct, with all team members making them a top priority in their calendars. The realities of the external world make this a difficult ideal to achieve — business pressures, the demands of higher management in the large organization and personal and family responsibilities of team members all conspire against its realization. If at all possible, meetings should go ahead as planned, with individual absences being accepted in exceptional circumstances.

Furthermore, these meetings (perhaps more than any others) require careful planning on the part of the individual who is going to be responsible for conducting them. This may be the team leader, but it does not have to be; he may delegate the task to a team member or bring in an external specialist as a facilitator. Using an outsider means that all team members, including the leader, can concentrate on the substance of the issues being discussed, leaving the process decisions to the specialist facilitator. If he knows his job, he runs the meeting in a way that maximizes the probability of each team member achieving his objectives, and the team as a whole leaves in better shape than that in which it arrived.

To do this, the facilitator needs to know in advance what each team member wants to achieve from the meeting, and they of course need to be clear themselves. When I am running a meeting of this kind (as an external specialist), I hold planning meetings with each individual, to explore the frame of mind in which they are coming to the meeting and the topics they wish to raise. In particular, I ask them to imagine themselves leaving the meeting extremely pleased with the event, and ask them, 'What would have to have happened for you to depart in that frame of mind?'

From these discussions, I obtain the information necessary to assess what might be achieved at the meeting and the chances of meeting the expectations of the participants in the time available. I have a sense of whether everyone is in fact coming to the same meeting, or whether it looks more like being a series of separate meetings. I also hope to have a feel for the emotional temperature of the group and any storms that are likely to blow up. (It is not, of course, an exact science — more like weather forecasting, in fact.)

It is now possible, in consultation with the team leader, to draw up an outline plan for the meeting, with the approximate time to be devoted to the various topics. I also have my own ideas as to the most appropriate techniques to be employed for different parts of the meeting. All of this, however, is a provisional plan only; events may well demand some instant changes of direction!

For most team meetings, an external facilitator is a luxury which cannot be afforded, but the same kind of planning as he would carry out needs to be undertaken by whoever assumes responsibility for running a meeting. If meetings are held fairly frequently, a standard format probably evolves to take care of routine matters, but meetings must not be allowed to become so routine that they turn into a mere formality.

What needs to be discussed is determined by the issues raised by team members, including the team leader. It is part of a team leader's action responsibility (which I cover in Chapter 4) to focus his team's attention on strategic issues — the team's mission or purpose (why it exists as a team at all); its strategies for fulfilling its mission; its values and means of operation.

This is a most important point, for it is the shared objectives and values which distinguish the permanent, or core, team from the temporary teams which each individual forms with the external people he interacts with on a win–win basis. It is these shared objectives and values, articulated as an exciting vision of the future, that mobilize the emotional energy and commitment of team members.

For the formulation of strategy to have this emotional impact, it must obviously be a participative process, even though initiated and ultimately controlled by the team leader. In participating, every member of the team has the opportunity, and the responsibility, to contribute his thoughts, wishes, ideas and opinions about the future of the team. It does *not* mean that every member has the right to *decide* about the future.

A business team (or any other team which exists in order to achieve anything in the real world) is *not* a democracy, in the sense of one man, one vote. Nor can it operate on the basis of everyone agreeing to everything. Teams that try to work in that way remind me of wartime convoys, proceeding at the speed of the slowest ships, their members huddled together for mutual protection!

On the contrary, the ultimate decisions on strategic matters fall within the action responsibility of the team leader. A leader is most unwise to go ahead without the broad support of team members for the direction he is taking, but he does not need (nor should he seek) the endorsement of each team member for each step of the way.

A team member who finds himself fundamentally out of sympathy with where his team is going, after offering his divergent views unsuccessfully to his colleagues and leader, has to decide whether it is still a team he wants to belong to. If this is so, he must sign on wholeheartedly to the strategy in spite of his reservations.

Equally, a leader who cannot get support for a strategy he wants to pursue has to develop an alternative strategy – or find another team or another job! A team can only work if all members know where they are going and are committed to getting there.

The fourth way in which autonomous individuals act together as an effective permanent team is through their caring for one another, particularly on a day-to-day basis. The whole question of interpersonal relationships within a team is so crucial to its success that it is examined in depth in Chapter 3. Here I want to draw attention to some of the kinds of behaviour that differentiate relationships between colleagues in a permanent team from those between members of a temporary team (however win–win those latter relationships may be).

Between close colleagues there is sharing at the emotional level as well as the functional. They rejoice in each other's successes and commiserate with each other's setbacks. There is a logic in doing so, because individuals' success contributes to a team's success, provided objectives are properly aligned. But there is more than logic: to provide emotional support when it is most needed is an important *raison d'être* for a team. It is one of the dimensions that make a team more than a collection of individuals.

Such emotional support can be forthcoming only when relationships within the team are based on the win–win principle. It cannot co-exist with internal competition of the win–lose variety. There is a place for healthy competition, of the kind that sets new and higher standards and stimulates emulation. (As I write, my own position as principal business-getter for my team is under severe threat from two younger members who are achieving previously unheard of levels of success. For me, it is a source of delight, while at the same time I strive to raise my game to meet the new standards they have set.)

Finally, autonomous members of a team work on a basis of mutual trust – or the assumption that each is working to the best of his abilities, knowledge and emotional condition to achieve his own and the team's objectives (the two being mutually compatible). Trust is a delicate plant which grows from shared positive experience of each other's behaviour, particularly under difficult circumstances. It can quickly be destroyed by a single let-down, real or perceived. A valuable guideline for team members is, 'Assume constructive intent' on the part of colleagues, particularly when things go wrong. Adherence to this in a particular situation ensures that an otherwise instant negative reaction is replaced by a positive attempt to explore what actually happened and why, and it is generally revealed that, although someone may have been mistaken (and to err is human), his intentions were honourable, and trust is not damaged.

Confidence in a person's judgement or wisdom may be damaged, but confidence is not the same thing as trust. You can send me out to play golf with Jack Nicklaus and *trust* me to give everything I've got, but you should not be *confident* that I will win!

How much teamwork?

It is easy to assume that because a number of executives report to the same boss, that group automatically constitutes a team and should behave like one. This assumption has been challenged effectively by Bill Critchley and David Casey, who take the view that 'there is a very *large* proportion of most managers' work where teamwork is not needed (and to attempt to inculcate teamwork is dysfunctional). There is at the same time a very *small* proportion of their work where teamwork is absolutely vital (and to ignore teamworking skills is to invite disaster).*

They go on to distinguish three modes of working which call for different kinds of interaction and different degrees of sharing, as follows:

*'Second Thoughts on Team Building', *Management Education and Development*, vol. 15, pt 2, pp. 163–75, 1984.

— Unshared certainty, applicable to most routine work in which issues are independent of each other. The 'mind your own business' principle applies, and the only interactions are polite social processes.

— Co-operation, for dealing with more complex issues that impinge on several members of a group. Here the interactive problem-solving methods described earlier, and the open-minded communication skills that go with them, are particularly appropriate. I would call this 'functional' teamwork, in which individuals still restrict their judgements to their own area of action responsibility but engage in interactive problem-solving to resolve conflicts and reach compatible solutions.

— Shared uncertainty, for major problems, perhaps concerning strategy, about which nobody knows what to do. A group is dealing here with the future and trying to create something new. There are no future facts (because it has not yet happened); past experience and expertise are of doubtful relevance. Personal feelings (which do not normally enter into management discussions) become highly relevant, if only because people are most likely to achieve what they most *want* to achieve. How to voice these feelings (and to what extent it is desirable to do so) is a crucial issue which I address below. This mode of working might be labelled (with some hesitation) 'emotional teamwork'. (Casey and Critchley, as well as other professional teambuilders, feel this is the only mode they can accept as 'real' teamwork!)

Distinguishing between these three modes of working is valuable because it enables us to apply the appropriate processes and techniques to the task in hand. Most management groups move between all three modes, though there is a tendency to avoid shared uncertainty by resorting to such ploys as appointing a consultant or setting up a task force. Furthermore, each mode finds its precise counterpart in the concepts of action responsibility and 'mind your own business' described earlier. Unshared certainty corresponds to the individual's area of autonomy; co-operation corresponds to interactive problem-solving; shared uncertainty is the characteristic of team objectives and strategy meetings.

My experience is that these meetings can be run very successfully using creative problem-solving techniques, with emphasis on creative techniques such as metaphor, analogy, scenario-writing, imaging and vision-building. These methods elicit the expression of feelings indirectly, and most managers can handle this comfortably. In fact, they can choose how far they will disclose their personal feelings, and I believe it is right that this should be a matter of personal choice.

The alternative approach, much favoured by professional psychologists and psychotherapists, is to *start* with feelings, to engage in what Casey and Critchley appropriately label 'soul-searching'. As they point out, 'Some people will argue that management groups cannot even begin to engage with each other in any kind of serious work . . . until they have first built a degree of openness and trust.' They go on, rightly in my opinion, to reject this approach, on the grounds that most management groups are likely to be task-centred and work at an intellectual rather than an emotional level. 'Approaching such a group suddenly at an emotional level will either generate shock, pain, distrust and confusion, or produce a warm, cosy, euphoric one-off experience', neither of which achieves anything of lasting value.

I believe that building openness and trust is a slow, patient and essentially gradual process, founded on a high level of interpersonal skill and supportive behaviour and regular, participative team meetings. The shared experiences of business successes and setbacks, reviewed and discussed constructively, create the bonds of trust gradually over the years.

Trust created in this way can in fact bring its own problems. It is clearly strongest among the longest-serving members of a team, who tend to develop an almost telepathic understanding of each other's views and reactions. This closeness can be resented by newcomers, who cannot belong to the charmed circle because there has not been time to develop the same kind of bond. They can easily feel excluded, and this feeling can have a divisive effect on a team.

I know of no easy solution to this problem. The inner group needs to be aware of the effect their cohesion can have, and try to remain open to the contributions of newcomers and sensitive to how it feels to be in their position. I have tried the 'soul-searching' approach with intra-group problems of this kind, using a skilled psychotherapist. On balance I believe the team benefited from it, though it certainly did not resolve all the problems and the team eventually decided to discontinue it. Certainly our business improved during that period, which suggests that the soul-searching was beneficial, but it has also continued to improve since we discontinued it!

3. Interpersonal relationships in the team

I referred at the beginning of the book to the correlation between team performance and team 'climate' or culture, the link being the amount of personal energy each individual had to use to protect himself from being hurt. Analysis of group behaviour from video-tapes has convinced me that individual self-esteem is fragile and easily damaged by any experience that is perceived as negative or punishing.

How team members manage their interpersonal relationships is a major factor affecting team climate (although not the only one – the quality of leadership, considered in Chapter 4, is also critical). In this chapter, I want to describe some guidelines and techniques I have found helpful in developing a code of practice for building sound personal relationships in a team. They represent 'work in progress'; I do not claim they are complete, but they might provide a starting point from which your own team can build a code of practice.

Some of the points raised (such as the 'mind your own business' principle) have been mentioned elsewhere and are repeated here for completeness.

Direct dealing

The principle of direct dealing is that any problem which arises between two team members is best dealt with directly by those individuals themselves, without the involvement of a third party, unless both are of the opinion that the presence of an agreed third party would be helpful. If they cannot resolve the issue on their own, it is the responsibility of *both* of them to refer the issue to their leader, together. (To have to do so reflects negatively on their interpersonal problem-solving skills and it should be very much a last resort.)

In day-to-day practice, this principle means that if Tom starts to complain to Dick about Harry's behaviour, Dick's most constructive response is, 'Talk to Harry about it, not me.' The worst thing Dick can do is to listen sympathetically and then go to see Harry himself and to reproach him with his behaviour towards Tom. Unfortunately there are a lot of well-meaning interfering busybodies who do just that!

Contrary to what Dick may think, it is *not* his business to act as a mediator between the two (unless they *both* ask him to, and they are in a bad way if they need to do that). It is *Tom's* responsibility as the aggrieved party to take the matter up directly with Harry; if he shirks that responsibility, Dick does nobody a favour by assuming it himself.

Moreover, Dick's intervention introduces 'noise' and distortion into the communication between Tom and Harry. Tom at least has first-hand knowledge of what he is upset about; Dick's information is necessarily second-hand and almost certainly not strictly accurate. By the time it reaches Harry, via Dick, it is third-hand and further distorted by Dick's interpretation of what he heard.

Interpersonal communication is difficult enough at the best of times; I have suggested elsewhere* that the typical success rate of face to face communication is 25 per cent, perhaps rising to 50 per cent among the more skilful. When the subject matter is emotive, the success rate falls. Communicating through a third party reduces it dramatically — it becomes 25 per cent of 25 per cent, i.e. 6.25 per cent! (Or at the very best, 50 per cent of 50 per cent, i.e. 25 per cent.)

The principle of direct dealing is simple in concept but more difficult in practice. It conflicts with the urge to gossip (i.e. to talk about someone behind his back and say things you would not say to his face). Gossip seems to be prevalent throughout society (hence the popularity of TV soap operas). It seems to bring drama and excitement into otherwise dull and boring lives. I believe it is wise to regard all gossip as potentially malicious in its effect, if not in intent; it has no place in a good team.

I will entertain, reluctantly, one possible exception to the direct

* In the companion volume, *Communication*.

dealing rule. It may be that Tom is so incensed by Harry's behaviour that he needs to let off steam to someone before he can talk rationally to Harry about it. He uses Dick as a sympathetic shoulder to cry on, before taking the matter up directly with Harry. If Dick restricts himself to listening sympathetically and calming Tom down without accepting the validity of his complaints (because he only has Tom's version of events), no harm is done. Dick has acted supportively, as a good team member should.

But who says that Tom has to talk *rationally* to Harry? Maybe it would be good feedback for Harry to experience at first hand just how upset Tom is? That depends on Harry's ability to cope with Tom's feelings without getting upset himself and the whole incident escalating into a blazing row. (Some would argue that the occasional blazing row does no harm to a team and should be seen as a sign of emotional honesty. This is not borne out by my experience, but perhaps that merely reflects on me – I hate emotional upheavals and would rather get on with the job.)

If Tom needs emotional support and a sympathetic ear, perhaps he can find it outside the team, at home, for example, or with a close friend or confidant. Here he is dealing with primarily emotional relationships, whereas relationships within a team, I believe, are primarily functional (albeit with an important emotional element). Not everyone agrees with this view, and I accept that there are grey areas between the concept of a team as a functional unit, with emotional dimensions, and the concept of a team as a therapy group existing to satisfy the emotional needs of its members (with which I have no sympathy).

Constructive feedback

In addition to dealing direct with interpersonal problems as they arise, team members also need to provide feedback on how they relate to each other on a more general basis. It would be unfortunate if they only discussed relationships when these were suffering, though too often this is what happens. When things are going well, we tend to take it for granted; as a result, all we ever get is the bad news.

Regular periodic reviews, on a semi-formal basis, keep a relationship in perspective and provide good learning opportunities for both parties. It requires some discipline to make sure they take place; the pressure of day-to-day events always seems more urgent, but putting in the relatively small amount of time required for a review is a necessary and rewarding investment.

For a team leader, a review at least annually with each team member constitutes a major part of his responsibilities. (It is probably required by the corporate appraisals system, though the kind of review I have in mind is very different from the traditional appraisal.) For other team members, the need for, and frequency of, review meetings depends on the extent of their interaction; it may make more sense for them to review specific shared experiences rather than their general relationship.

The format I favour for a review is that of a mutual problem-solving meeting. It starts with each individual delivering a detailed and balanced statement of his experience of working with the other, preferably prepared in advance to give time for sufficient depth of thought. The statement is in the form of an itemized response (in problem-solving jargon), i.e.:

— these are the things I appreciate, enjoy and admire in my experience of working with you – the positives;
— these are the aspects I wish we could change – the negatives, but expressed as directions for improvement and alteration.

This format is essential for feedback to be perceived as constructive. It is expressed in terms of information about the person giving the feedback; it is not meant to constitute , and is not expressed in terms of, objective information about the recipient. Consequently, it is likely to be accurate, and can be accepted as accurate – I am the expert on my experience of you, just as you are the expert on *your* experience of me.

It also allows for an exchange on a basis of equality – the same kind of information is given in both directions. This is particularly important when the team leader is involved in a review. He has special responsibilities as leader, but these do not make him a superior human being.

Identification of the positive features of a relationship provides a perspective for any discussion of possible improvements, and is critical to the constructive climate of a review. We all need to know what we are doing well, and we are too seldom told. When we are informed, we have a strong tendency to discount the good news. Why this should be so I am not sure, but I suspect that the massive amount of negative feedback we receive as children results in low self-esteem and a highly developed internal self-critic. The positives need to be heard, and it is useful to have the recipient paraphrase his understanding of them, without discounts.

The negatives are framed as wishes for improvement, i.e. problems to be solved. They are not criticisms (though they can easily be interpreted as such, given the tendency to self-criticism). They are concerned with the future, not the past, and they invite ideas for action by either party to improve the situation. Maybe there are things that I could do to help solve the problem I have identified. Unlike the conventional appraisal, there is no assumption that the responsibility for change lies only with the recipient of the feedback.

In fact, the problem areas identified by the two individuals are likely to be related – they are often both conscious of the same difficulties. Once identified, they can frequently be solved by applying relatively simple ideas. The solutions adopted should be written down in the form of a mutual contract, adherence to which it is hoped will ensure the desired improvement in the relationship. This provides a starting point for the next review – how far have we achieved what we agreed to do?; what still remains to be done?

A good review meeting is a win–win experience. (Compare this with the conventional appraisal!) Afterwards both parties feel better understood and better appreciated and they have agreed on what to do to improve their relationship. As the relationship develops, reviews become quicker and less formal. Eventually a level of trust and confidence may be reached at which formal reviews become redundant. As stepping-stones to that end, I have found them invaluable.

Incidentally, if you do have to carry out a standard appraisal, be assured that this sort of review meeting gives you all the information you need, at a much higher level than any other procedure I know!

Coaching/learning

The same feedback principles can be applied to the processes of learning from and coaching each other within a team. In my own team, in which we frequently have occasion to work in pairs and one person has the opportunity to observe another in action, it is standard practice for the observer to write 'coaching notes'. These represent his view of what happens and are accepted as such, without consideration of whether he is 'right' or 'wrong'. The subject's experience may well be different, and that is accepted too. We all see the world differently, and it is not unusual for two people to experience the same event differently.

Feedback is much more acceptable and useful if it is presented as information about the observer rather than a judgement about the observed. Differences of view then become interesting areas for exploration and learning on the part of both parties. Conversely, the same information presented as a judgement, e.g. 'The right way to do it is . . . or 'What you should do is . . .', is likely to provoke a defensive reaction, e.g. 'I did it that way because . . .', which can lead to argument and debate about who is right and who is wrong. On the other hand, the judgement may be apparently accepted but resented. Either reaction tends to close the mind to learning and diminish the value of the feedback.

Presenting a judgement has this effect because it sets up a superior–inferior relationship, leaving the recipient in an emotionally 'one-down' position, which is damaging to his self-esteem. His mind is likely to close as a means of protection against the pain.

Even though a coach may be vastly more experienced and knowledgeable than his 'student', he must bear in mind that the student's way may be right for him. Equally, a student is foolish to ignore his coach's greater experience and knowledge, but he does not have to behave as though his coach is infallible. A good sense of a productive relationship between coach and student is captured by Al Huang's definition of a master:

A master is someone who started before you did.*

A good coach provides a model of the learning process and must therefore be open to learning himself and demonstrate that this is the case. Again, therefore, feedback needs to be two-way. The observations of the less experienced person provide important information concerning his own learning process, indicating what points are registering with him and what are not. They also provide the coach with a mirror which reflects the effectiveness or otherwise of his coaching. They may also stimulate additions to the coach's own knowledge and awareness.

Conflicts

Just as a chain is only as strong as its weakest link, so a team is only as strong as its weakest interpersonal relationship. Where there is animosity and hostility between two members, or even mere

*Quoted in Gary Zukov, *The Dancing Wu Li Masters*, Hutchinson, 1979.

personal dislike, there is potential for divisiveness and a threat to team cohesion.

Warring parties tend to disagree almost automatically about everything, taking opposing points of view almost out of habit. They seek to recruit allies and in so doing extend their division through the team. Their antipathies close their minds to each other's ideas, blocking the way to the creative problem-solving needed to resolve substantive issues. Their animosity casts a shadow over the team climate, embarrassing other members and generating a state of 'psychic contamination'.

The frustrating thing about a situation like this is that nobody can really do much about it except the contestants themselves, and they may be unwilling or unable to do so. The team leader and other team members can offer to help or mediate; professional external help, perhaps from a psychotherapist, can be enlisted; work can be organized to minimize interaction between the parties concerned. At the end of the day, however, none of these remedies works unless the individuals want them to.

In the end, there is no course open to a team leader but to bang their heads together, tell them (preferably together) that their behaviour will no longer be tolerated and make it clear that they will *both* have to leave the team if they cannot settle their differences within a reasonable time. This at least gives them something in common – imminent departure from the team – and an incentive to sort themselves out!

A leader should not, in my opinion, allow either of the protagonists to drive the other out of the team. Nor should he allow himself to be set up as judge of which party is guilty and which innocent. It is up to each of them, as responsible team members, to manage their relationship constructively. They do not have to *like* each other, but they must develop a satisfactory way of working together and refrain from destructive behaviour. Failing this, they must leave.

Humour

By their jokes you will know them. A healthy team is a good-humoured team, one in which smiles and laughter are the order of the day. But the *quality* of the humour is all important.

Among the groups I work with, I frequently encounter a lot of leg-pulling and jokes at everyone's expense. it is perceived by group

39

members as a healthy, normal interaction — even a sign of good teamwork — and they are astonished when I challenge this view.

Over time, I have begun to see a correlation within groups between the prevalence of this kind of 'sharp' humour and of cautious, guarded behaviour when it comes to discussing work issues. Team members are reluctant to risk putting forward new ideas, or say what they really think or feel, for fear of being the butt of a colleague's wit. Though there may be laughter, it has an uncomfortable feel to it.

Undoubtedly this kind of humour sets up 'revenge cycles' — you make a crack at my expense and I am sure to get you back at the earliest possible moment. All good clean fun, I am told by the protagonists, but I am not convinced. At the very least, these revenge cycles take up energy that could be more usefully deployed on the job — I have to be on the alert to spot my opportunity to get back at you, and keep my guard up against your next thrust. It is certainly a distraction.

More seriously, it is a win–lose activity, and therefore contrary to the win–win approach that a team must adopt if it is to be a healthy one. Win–lose rapidly becomes lose–lose, as the loser of the first round sets up a return match on his own ground which he is sure to win.

I am aware that my view runs counter to much of our national culture, particularly that of the north of England (including my home town of Liverpool!) in which the ability to give and receive sharp knocks is prized as a sign of maturity. (It is even more pronounced in Australia.) But there are other societies, in Europe, America and the East, which do not seem to need this kind of humour and, I suspect, get on better without it.

My reason for asserting this is quite simple: however good-natured the *intent* of the joke-maker, the effect on the recipient is very likely to be negative. He may not be aware of the hurt he receives, and consequently not acknowledge it, but watch his subsequent behaviour (preferably a few times on videotape) and you can see his guardedness and desire to get his own back, resulting from the blow to his self-esteem.

With some reluctance I have tried to curb my own tendency to make fun of others; I have decided it is too dangerous and too costly. There is enough to laugh about in the world around us without laughing at each other!

'Mind your own business'

In voicing this apparently 'hostile' expression I am in fact urging respect for the autonomy of team members. It means making sure a colleague wants to hear your ideas and opinions concerning what he is doing before you actually offer them, i.e. not interfering without permission, however helpful you feel your interference is going to be. It is up to him to decide whether he wants his work to be interfered with or not!

An important corollary of this principle is to speak for yourself. You are the expert on you and can speak with authority about yourself. The same applies to all individuals. It follows that I cannot speak with authority about what anyone else is thinking or feeling; I can only speak about *my perception*, of these things, a very different matter.

It is also dangerous to presume to speak for someone else by classing them under the collective 'we'. It must be clear who 'we' represents in addition to the speaker. Have the other parties mandated the speaker to speak for them? If not, he is only entitled to speak for himself, to use 'I', not 'we'.

The use of 'we' (and its close associate 'one') can cause a lot of subtle trouble in working groups. It creates situations in which members of a group are conscripted by a speaker to a view he is expressing, without their consent. They are faced with the choice of going along with it or voicing their opposition, neither of which they may want to do. This can happen so quickly they are not aware of what is going on and suddenly find themselves identified with a position they do not support.

Of course there are times when 'we' is appropriate – for example, in the expression of agreed corporate policy ('We only give refunds on production of a receipt.') But many people say 'we' when they have the right only to say 'I', and in so doing muddy the waters of team relationship.

Assume constructive intent

Any transaction between two individuals is not one event but two – it represents a different experience for each of the individuals concerned. Looked at in this way, many misapprehensions and breakdowns in interpersonal relationships become readily understandable. Two people's experience of the same event can differ enormously, in a manner quite unanticipated by the initiator of that event.

When intent and effect are uncoupled in this manner, it is common to find that positively intended actions have a negative effect. Maybe they are undertaken unwisely or carried out clumsily, or maybe the recipient misunderstands or is hypersensitive. My experience is that people seldom set out to hurt each other (unless they are already locked into a long-standing feud). Damage is the result of clumsiness rather than malice.

Once this hypothesis is accepted, it is possible to place a negative experience in a different perspective. Suppose the initiator of a particular transaction, the effect of which is perceived by a recipient as destructive, had in mind something constructive, what might this have been? Such an approach is a positive response to the assumed constructive intent, not a negative reaction to the apparent negative effect.

If, for example, you say to me, 'Your idea won't work. We tried it a couple of years ago and it flopped', I can reply, 'That's only because you bungled it.' (i.e. get my revenge). Conversely, assuming constructive intent, I can say, 'It sounds as if you had an experience a couple of years ago that you consider relevant. I'd like to hear more about it.' The door is now open to constructive discussion of how my idea might be modified to avoid the fate of two years previously.

To be able to manage immediate emotional reaction (sit on it, in fact) long enough to explore the probable constructive intent behind what causes it, is an invaluable skill in a team. It creates a calm and positive emotional climate and saves endless time and energy otherwise wasted in unnecessary wrangling. Its effective exercise calls for a high degree of emotional maturity, and it is a leader's responsibility to set an example. However, he probably has less need of recourse to this skill than other team members; he is, after all, less likely to be the subject of attack on account of his position as leader. Rather, older and more experienced members of a team might be better placed to set an example, although in my experience there is no necessary correlation between age and emotional maturity!

4. Team leadership

The concept of team leader

Almost implicit in the idea of a team is the assumption that it has a leader of some kind, a captain, manager or coach, to name but a few commonly employed titles. (A football team may have all three of these, each assuming a distinct role.)

What is involved in taking on the role of leader varies according to a team's activities. A cricket captain makes, and takes responsibility for, strategic decisions, such as whether or not to bat on winning the toss, or whether to declare an innings closed rather than continue batting. He also makes tactical decisions, on such matters as which bowlers to use, from which end they are best deployed and when it is most expedient to change them, and in which order his players go into bat.

A football captain, on the other hand, can do no more (on the field of play) than lead by example and cajole, encourage and exhort those within earshot – an altogether less powerful role.

In a work context, a team leader usually bears the title 'manager', and his immediate team consists of those who report directly to him. His leadership responsibilities extend beyond this, however, to all the sub-teams in his part of the organization. Each member of his immediate team may well lead their own team, the pattern continuing up and down the hierarchy. Every manager (except the chief executive) is both a team leader and a member of another, higher level team.

Like Janus, therefore, a manager faces two ways, and his two roles may call for quite different behaviours. He is confronted with the difficult task of looking in opposite directions without appearing two-faced (or developing a split personality!). His responsibilities are likely to cover *all* the functions of sports captains noted above, and a few more besides. Typically, he is responsible for:

— making certain specific decisions;
— maintaining team morale;
— leading by example;
— team selection;
— allocation of responsibilities and resources;
— coaching, i.e. developing the skills of team members;
— stimulating a sense of purpose and excitement about the future – the feeling that his is a great team to belong to because it is going to do great things.

It is a formidable and possibly daunting list. Consideration of these responsibilities can easily create the feeling that they are beyond the scope of the average manager and call for a special kind of supermanager. There do, of course, exist some specially gifted individuals who take to them like a duck to water (the action profiles described in Chapter 5 can help to identify them). But I believe it is well within the scope of the averagely gifted manager competently to fulfil the role of leader, once he is aware of the nature of that role and what it requires of him.

A number of considerations, however, can ease the burden. A team leader is not alone. He can look to his own boss for guidance and support, unless he happens to be the chief executive, in which case he may turn to a trusted external confidant, perhaps a non-executive director or consultant.

His team members can also be a source of support, given a relationship between him and them that is based on mutual respect *and* a mutual recognition and acceptance of his distinctive role and authority. To establish such a relationship in the first place is one of his primary tasks.

When a team leader takes his place within a large organization, major strategic decisions have (it is to be hoped!) been taken already. A company, assuming it is reasonably well led from the top, has already defined its corporate mission, and devised the strategy by which this is to be fulfilled. It has also articulated its value system (although, as we have seen, this tends to be a blind spot for many British companies!).

Assuming a company has done a reasonable job in these areas, an individual team leader's strategies become a subset of the corporate strategy, and the strategic decisions he has to take are fairly straightforward and need only be checked out with his boss.

Under these circumstances, and assuming he has the technical competence to handle the job, neither the strategic nor the tactical decision-making aspects of his work should cause him much difficulty. He is free to concentrate his energy on the development of interpersonal relationships within his team, the area in which success or failure as a leader is ultimately determined.

If, however, there is no corporate strategy, a team leader must take on the role of the entrepreneur – the leader of an independent team – and seize the opportunity to develop his own strategy. This is the ideal vehicle for creating an exciting vision of the future which mobilizes the energy and commitment of a team.

Recently I worked with a team of educational psychologists employed by a local education authority. One of their problems, they complained, was that the authority had no clear strategy for the role of educational psychologists in the education system. To me this seemed to be the ideal opportunity for *them* to work out what they believed the strategy should be, and start putting it into practice. At best, they would have the strategy they wanted; at worst, they would provoke a reaction which would lead to the development of an alternative strategy, thereby filling the vacuum of which they were complaining. Either way it would be an exciting project with shared risks and shared benefits, a perfect way to build a high-performance team.

Developing your leadership skills

If you are one of nature's born leaders, this section has nothing to offer you; you do it all, intuitively, and no doubt more besides. However, before you move on, it might be worth answering the question, 'How do you know you are a born leader?' I have known a few people who prided themselves on their leadership skills, but their team members told a very different story!

It might be worth getting some objective feedback before concluding that your leadership style has no scope for improvement. One way of doing this is to ask an independent observer, like an external consultant, who can talk to team members individually and report back the collective view while preserving the anonymity of individual comments. Alternatively, you can use a structured questionnaire, such as the one developed by Roger Harrison and

David Berlew of Situation Management Inc. in connection with their Power and Influence Programme.

Not being a born leader myself, I cannot claim to know the precise formula of leadership, but I think it is worth sharing the conclusions I have formed from my own experience of leadership and observation of a wide variety of leaders at work. The following principles seem to me to be important:

— *Be yourself:* you can only lead in ways that come naturally to you. It is fatal to keep in mind an image of what you think a leader should be and to try to live up to that if doing so involves putting on an act. Your team members are not stupid; they know when they are being conned (even if they do not know *how*). Your personal integrity is your most valuable asset and the basis of the trust you need to build with your team. Do not put it at risk by acting a part.

— *Know yourself:* if you have a clear idea of what you do well naturally, and where you are vulnerable, you can structure your activity as leader to exploit your strengths and get help where you need it. I find that knowledge of my own action profile is a great help in this respect, and I imagine that other forms of psycho-metric measurement would serve the same purpose if they were reasonably accurate.

— *Define your role as leader:* your team needs to know what kind of activities you are going to engage in as leader, and what decisions you are going to make. They need to know in which areas they have the autonomy to make their own decisions, when they need to get your approval for what they want to do, and when you reserve decision-making for yourself. Similarly, they need to know which of your policies are fixed and non-negotiable, and which are open to discussion and change. People need to know where they stand; to know that, they need to know where *you* stand, and it is your job to tell them.

— *Provide a model of behaviour you want practised in the team:* you are the architect and the guardian of the team's style of working, and the team takes its cue from the example you set. If you believe it is important that meetings start on time, for example, you have to be on time yourself (normally – you are allowed some human frailty, too!)

— *Come clean:* you have to disclose what you are thinking and planning to do. If you do not, your team members only waste their energy guessing and adjusting their behaviour accordingly – and they can easily guess wrongly. Of course, there are times when you have information you are not at liberty to disclose because it has

46

been given to you in confidence, but your need to acknowledge the fact ('This is the way it's going to be, for reasons I'm not in a position to disclose.') Your personal honesty is essential to the building of trust, and if you want honesty in a team you have to set an example yourself.

— *Give constructive feedback:* I have already emphasized (see Chapter 3) the critical importance of feedback being given in ways that recognize the sensitivity of the recipient and enable him to do something positive with it. In particular, be generous with your appreciation: it costs you nothing, but is of inestimable value to the recipient in building his self-esteem. Some managers work on the opposite principle: 'He is a professional. Why should I praise him for doing the job he is paid to do? I will tell him only when he falls short.' As well as being mean-spirited, this is a short-sighted, self-defeating approach. It assumes that a leader and team members have identical views on what the requirements of a job are (a dangerous assumption) and means that all news is bad news (the most effective demotivator imaginable!)

— *Give honours judiciously:* 'What is honoured in a country is what is practised there.' Any promotions, commendations or other awards you hand out are interpreted by team members, quite rightly, as evidence of your value system. They adapt their behaviour accordingly. If a team member is rewarded for successful performance achieved by dubious methods, the message is, 'Dubious methods are okay as long as they bring results.' That may be the message you want to give, but it would be a pity to give it inadvertently!

— *Be consistent:* few things are more demoralizing to members of a team than to find that the goal posts have been moved without warning. They have been working to achieve success by one set of criteria and find themselves being judged by a different set. The criteria by which you judge people need to be explicit and stable.

I am conscious that the whole philosophy of leadership underlying these principles runs counter to what might be called the 'tough management' school of thought. This is based on the belief that people at work are motivated primarily by fear, and is expressed in such maxims as 'Divide and rule', 'Keep them guessing', 'Make them compete against each other.' It has to be said that some exponents of this philosophy have successful track records to support it.

The issue for me is whether these people are successful because of their philosophy or in spite of it. I believe they would be even more successful following my principles, but we have no way of testing who is right. However, I do not accept that my way need be any less 'tough' than theirs; on the contrary, objectives can be just as demanding and standards just as high. The difference is that these matters are out in the open, and everyone knows where they stand. For me, that in itself is a huge benefit; it is the way I prefer to live and work, and I would be willing to trade some commercial success for it if that were necessary. But I do not believe it is!

I am convinced (though, again, I have no proof) that the more the environment a team works in requires innovation, and the greater the extent of external change, the more team members need a style of leadership that is open, honest and constructive. In conditions of great uncertainty, there is no way of knowing whether a particular initiative is going to be successful or not. Team members have to have the confidence that they can take sensible (i.e. affordable) risks without being penalized if they are not successful.

If they lack the confidence to do this, they refer all risky decisions to their team leader, who is probably less well placed than they are to take them because he is further from the action and therefore less well informed. Then the leader complains of being overloaded and burdened with unenterprising subordinates!

Team members should be encouraged to check with their leader before taking serious risks, and the leader, while having the right of veto, should share responsibility if he decides these risks are to be taken. An environment which prompts such behaviour is created only through trust and mutual respect.

Leadership and democracy

There is a widespread belief, especially among younger people and in the public, as opposed to the private, sector, that teams should be 'democratic'. What is meant by 'democratic' in the context of a working team is not too clearly defined, but it seems to imply everyone having the right to have a say in every decision that affects them. If there is disagreement, as is almost inevitable, decisions are presumably taken by vote!

I believe that this view is based on a false notion of democracy; it also happens to be unworkable in practice. Political democracy champions the principle of one man, one vote. Having elected a government, the electorate has to accept that the government will make its own decisions without consulting it further until the next election, as a result of which it may be replaced. Even in that most democratic institution, the sports club, members elect the team captain. Once elected, the captain makes his own decisions, with as much or as little consultation as he sees fit, until such time as the members decide to elect someone else to the job.

Similarly, in a workers' co-op or common ownership company, members, in their capacity as owners of the business, appoint or elect the management (in the same way that shareholders theoretically elect the directors of a limited liability company). Once appointed, management leads the business in the way it sees fit. This includes taking unpopular decisions because it believes them to be right for the success of the business. Whether it is re-elected or not should depend on the performance of the business under its leadership, not on whether it interprets correctly the wishes of its constituents on every issue!

I recently worked with a team leader who told me that he saw himself as *primus inter pares* ('first among equals', he translated, to make sure I got the point). He refused to give a lead on anything, complained about poor standards of work, criticized his subordinates and refused to take responsibility for anything himself. Not surprisingly his team ran around in circles like a bunch of headless chickens, making a lot of noise and achieving very little. Where they needed leadership there was a vacuum.

'First among equals' is a helpful concept if it is taken to mean that everyone in a team is equal in terms of deserving the same degree of respect and identical treatment (analogous to 'equal before the law' in a democratic society). But members of a work team do different jobs, and a leader has a unique job that only he can do. 'First among equals' is not an excuse to abdicate the responsibilities of leadership.

Situational leadership

'Situational leadership' is the label given by management researchers Paul Hersey and Ken Blanchard to the unsurprising assertion that 'there is no single all-purpose leadership style. Successful leaders are those who can adapt their behaviour to meet the demands of their own unique situations.' As a general proposition, this is hardly news to practising managers. (It is more of a surprise to management academics, who have apparently been involved in a search for the 'best' style of management for some decades!) However, the Hersey–Blanchard model usefully goes on to identify three variables which provide some clues as to *how* a leader should vary his style according to his situation. Two of the variables relate to the leader's style and the third to the capacity of the 'follower' (the party that is led).

The two leader variables are called 'task behaviour' and 'relationship behaviour', and are defined by Hersey and Blanchard as follows:

Task behaviour is the extent to which a leader engages in one-way communication by explaining what each follower has to do as well as when, where and how tasks are to be accomplished.

Relationship behaviour is the extent to which a leader engages in two-way communication by providing socio-emotional support, 'psychological strokes', and facilitating behaviours.

These are identified as two independent variables which can co-exist in a leader's style to any degree, as opposed to either–or elements which exist only in a single continuum (so that a manager is described as either predominantly task-oriented *or* relationship-oriented). In the Hersey–Blanchard model he can be both (or either!) – a breakthrough for common-sense!

This distinction allows the authors to draw one of those quadrant diagrams beloved of management writers, dividing leadership style into four categories:

— high task and low relationship;
— high task and high relationship;
— high relationship and low task;
— low relationship and low task.

('High' and 'low' relate to the *degree* of each type of behaviour exhibited by a leader, rather than its nature!) Any of these styles may be effective, depending on the 'situation'. This is defined in terms of the degree of 'maturity' of a follower in relation to a specific task. Someone new to a task obviously needs more direction and guidance than someone familiar with it. More controversially, Hersey and Blanchard suggest that a newcomer needs less 'socio-emotional' support than an established follower (or is it that a leader, in spelling out to a newcomer what a task entails, has no time or energy for supportive behaviour?)

Be that as it may, the four leadership styles are mapped on to the degree of task-relevant maturity of followers in order to ascertain which of them has the highest probability of carrying out successfully which particular jobs, as follows:

— *Telling* (high task/low relationship): leader simply issues instructions;

— *Selling* (high task/high relationship): leader still makes the decisions but tries to persuade his followers to support them;
— *Participating* (high relationship/low task): leader and followers share decision-making;
— *Delegating* (low relationship/low task): leader lets followers do the job their own way, because they are willing and able to do so.

Thus, the situational leadership theory calls for a high degree of flexibility on the part of a leader. He may need to vary his approach with the same individual on different tasks, with different individuals on the same task, and with the same individual over time as his maturity and competence in a particular area increase. This is a disturbing proposition for a leader who has evolved a style of his own which he uses all the time!

I would say that if you have a personal style that works for you, stay with it until you come across a situation in which it does not work. Then look to this model for some clue as to where you may be going wrong and how you might usefully modify your approach. You may find it particularly relevant when you move into a new job or get promoted (remembering the Peter Principle, which states that people tend to be promoted to their level of incompetence, i.e. the level at which their habitual style is no longer appropriate and they fail to modify it).

While a model of this kind is a useful tool to clarify the issues involved and provide a common language for their discussion, I have reservations about some of the implications of this particular one. There is potential for conflict with at least two of the leadership principles put forward earlier, viz. 'Be yourself' and 'Be consistent.'

If it does not come naturally to you to engage in high relationship behaviour, do not try to force it. If you do, it will appear insincere and possibly patronizing, and will do more harm than good. Paradoxically, a *small* move in that direction may well have a powerful impact if you are known as habitually reserved. People will be aware of the effort it has cost you!

The demand for consistency may well be met by telling your team that you intend to operate on the Hersey–Blanchard principles. The only issue then remaining is that of securing agreement on individuals' levels of maturity as regards particular tasks, which is a subject for discussion between you. In the last analysis, it is your judgement as leader that counts, since you carry ultimate responsibility for the performance of the team as a whole.

At a more fundamental level, the model fails to take into account the *quality* of relationships between a leader and his team members.

If the level of mutual respect and trust is sufficiently high, the varying degrees of competence in respect of different tasks present no problem. A team member actively seeks help and welcomes guidance and direction when he is working on something new or something he finds difficult.

When his task-relevant maturity is low, a team member is at his most vulnerable and therefore in need of the maximum socio-emotional support his leader can lend, as well as the maximum direction and guidance. As he becomes more competent he may need less of both in purely quantitative terms, but the quality of relationship must be sustained at the highest level right across the spectrum.

I am also suspicious of the idea of a leader 'selling' a decision to a team. It smacks of manipulation and phony consultation. It is his privilege to decide which issues he settles on his own, with or without prior consultation, and which he tackles in a participative manner. In many situations he may be well-advised to consult first and obtain feedback on a proposal before coming to a final decision. He is also well-advised to give his reasons for reaching a particular decision whenever possible. At the end of the day, of course, a decision is his; team members who do not like it must either accept it or leave the team.

There is one other situational variable that has a major bearing on the appropriateness of leadership style. This is the nature of a team's activities, broadly classifiable as 'operational' or 'developmental'. In an operational situation a team operates in real time, and many decisions have to be made instantly; the situation is probably a routine one for which there are known solutions and drills. Developmental activity is concerned with the future: there remains time for consultation and for exploration of a variety of options, and there is likely to be a call for a high degree of original thinking.

In general, an operational situation calls for a decisive leadership style (and a corresponding instant response from team members). In developmental activity, a consultative style is more appropriate – no one knows the answers, and there is time to search for them.

The same team may operate in both kinds of situation at different times. Thus a fire brigade crew fighting a fire is in operational mode and autocratic leadership from the captain is called for. On the following day, the same crew might discuss ways of improving its firefighting techniques for the future, and a highly participative mode is then appropriate.

Perhaps the ideal leadership style is one which is flexible and allows a leader to adapt his approach according to the precise demands of a situation (within the natural limits of a leader's personality), with both leader and team members being clear about the basis on which the flexibility is being exercised. I hasten to add that I have not yet reached this nirvana myself!

The leader as coach

It is fashionable nowadays to view the development of a leader's subordinates as one of his principal responsibilities, so that as well as being a manager he is also a coach. Because a leader is usually older, more experienced and it is to be hoped, wiser than those he leads, the idea has immediate appeal. Moreover, if a leader sees himself a a coach, he is less likely to interfere to the point of doing a job himself. Even so, because the perception of a leader as a coach is so fashionable, it is worth taking a critical look at it.

Why *should* a leader take responsibility for the development of team members? What benefit does he, the team or the organization gain from his doing so? How about team members taking responsibility for their own development? What about the role of the management development manager in the personnel department?

The answers are different for an independent team and a team that is part of a larger organization. In the case of an independent team, the growth of the people in it drives the growth of the business itself, or at the very least limits its capacity for growth. For the leader, investment of his time and energy in the development of his team members is an investment in the future of the business – assuming they stay in the business. And they are more likely to stay if they feel they are improving their skills and amassing relevant experience. The coaching relationship inevitably brings the leader and individual team member into close personal contact, and this helps the leader keep his finger on the pulse of team morale.

Many of the same benefits can be reaped by a team within a larger organization, but space for expansion of its activities cannot be taken for granted. If this is lacking, the development of team members can lead to frustration on the part of the individuals concerned and the temptation on the part of the team to empire-build or encroach on other teams' spheres of activity.

Moreover, there is often a trade-off between developing people in a team and achieving short-term results. Development takes time and energy and involves risks in giving tasks to inexperienced people that would be done quicker and better by someone already experienced. If a team leader is to be judged by short-term results, he needs to think hard about investing in the long term – he may not be there to enjoy the rewards! (An ambitious team leader may not intend to be there – his strategy may be to get himself promoted by achieving visible short-term results without regard to the long-term consequences! Being a coach has no place in such a strategy!)

For the leader of a team within an organization, the extent of his responsibility for developing his subordinates needs to be worked out explicitly and agreed with his boss. It cannot be taken for granted. Maybe the organization wants to use his department as a training ground for future managers of other parts of the business. If so, it must be made an explicit objective.

Furthermore, a leader's ability to be a good coach cannot be assumed. A person is often appointed leader because of his success as a performer of his team's activities (or one of them), but the best performers tend not to be good coaches. They may not know how they achieve their results; they may just do it instinctively. It probably comes easily to them, so they have little understanding of, or patience with, the difficulties of the less gifted.

It is, in fact, unreasonable to expect any team leader to be an effective coach without providing him with relevant training. A coach is, or should be, a facilitator of learning. This is a very different concept from that of the traditional teacher, on which most managers unconsciously model themselves in tackling their coaching duties. A teacher is perceived as a source of knowledge (often information) which is to be passed on to pupils; the criterion of success is often the pupils' ability to regurgitate the same information in an examination.

The role of coach is one of helping pupils develop their ability to do new things. It is a process of skill development, in which the active role is that of the learner, not the coach. The coach facilitates this process by setting up the learning opportunities, ideally in a series of graduated steps of increasing difficulty, and by giving feedback at each stage in a helpful way. In the real world, as opposed to a training environment, it is not so easy to prov de a series of suitably graded steps. The approach has to be much more opportunist, and a team leader has to judge when to throw someone in at the deep end, and when he does so, what support to provide. If his team operates in an environment of innovation, circumstances often make these decisions for him; when no one has previous experience of a situation, it provides an opportunity for everybody to learn!

Ideally the steps should be so graduated that each one is a stretch, but can be accomplished successfully, and if it is not, the consequences are acceptable. (It needs a stable environment to be able to get close to this ideal – where innovation is taking place it is unlikely to be possible). The aim is to build confidence through successful achievement of progressively more difficult tasks. The experience of these achievements is the essence of the learning process; feedback provides reinforcement of the experience.

For feedback to be experienced as reinforcement, it must be positive, constructive and forward-looking. In the process of experiential learning, any experience is received in a positive fashion, in that it is recognized as providing the material for learning, regardless of its consequences. Indeed, the more unexpected the consequences, the greater the potential for learning.

A leader's reaction to what goes wrong is all-important. If he reacts to every setback as to a major disaster, his feedback is experienced as negative and punishing. Consequently his team develops an aversion to risk-taking and innovation, and ceases to learn.

'We have a monumental cock-up on our hands,' said Fred, the international production director of a multinational company. The occasion was his annual conference of production directors from subsidiaries around the world, being held this time in Madrid. The monumental cock-up? Fred had discovered that slide projectors in Spain take a different sized slide from those he had brought from the US! He can choose to see this as a challenge to his ingenuity, and tackle the question of how to get his message over without his slides, or how to adapt his slides to fit the projector, or how to find an American-sized projector in Madrid! He could also have seen it as an interesting learning experience for himself, the discovery that American slides (like American stationery sizes, weights and measures) are not standard with those elsewhere in the world. But Fred chose to see it as the result of a blunder by the Spanish production director, who was hosting the conference – an unfair and demotivating reaction, in my opinion.

When something goes wrong, there are only two things you can usefully do – find ways to put it right and learn from the experience for future reference. To learn from it you may have to conduct an inquiry into what went wrong and why, but if an inquiry turns into a witch-hunt with the object of apportioning blame, it generates a cover up and nothing is learned. Apportioning blame is only worthwhile if a disaster is so serious that you have to get rid of the people responsible for it.

Not long ago I was comparing experiences with my opposite number in the US. I mentioned that it was some years since we had had a client session that went seriously wrong. Their experience had been the same, he said. There was a pause, then he went on: 'I'm not so sure that's such a good thing. It probably means we're not taking enough risks. When a session did go wrong, we used to research the hell out of it, and we learned a lot from it!'

By adopting this sort of attitude, a leader really does establish an environment that is conducive to learning, and in so doing establishes his role as coach. By inviting and welcoming feedback (provided it is positive, constructive and forward-looking!) and acting upon it, he demonstrates his own readiness to learn, thereby setting an example to his team. The two-way appraisals described in Chapter 3 provide an excellent opportunity for a leader to engage in mutual learning with team members and to demonstrate his own willingness to learn and change.

'Followership'

A great deal is said and written about 'leadership', yet 'followership' is rarely mentioned. The existence of one implies the existence of the other: it would be an odd sort of leader who had no followers!

Intuitively and emotionally I (and, I suspect, others in the field) back away from the notion of 'followership', because it suggests subservience and loss of dignity – it has a sheep-like ring to it. But the issue cannot be fudged; quite simply there are many more followers than leaders, and as we have already seen, every leader in a hierarchical organization (except the chief executive) is also a follower, a member of a higher level team than the one he leads. How can he fulfil these two apparently opposing roles without detriment to his own consistency and integrity as a human being?

I remember sitting talking to Arthur, the chief executive of the UK subsidiary of an American-owned multinational company, when a call came through from the company president in the US. Instantly, the powerful, authoritative, even dominating personality I had been talking to was transformed into a crawling, subservient creep! I was astonished, and began to see why his subordinates did not hold him in the same high regard as that in which I had been inclined to hold him!

The paradox resolves itself if we go back to the concept of action responsibility (see Chapter 2) and the notion of a contract between an individual and an organization. By joining an organization, or by moving into a particular job within it (and so joining a particular team), an individual enters into a contract with the organization – he is bound to carry out certain tasks and accept certain constraints. This contract defines the space within which he exercises his action responsibility; it is his area of autonomy.

In an organization there is a hierarchy of activities, in that the higher level activities constrain the lower level ones. A leader is responsible for higher level activities and in fulfilling his responsibility constrains his followers. If he is skilful, he does this without diminishing the motivation of team members; ideally this is enhanced through a process of consultation and mutual problem-solving.

Obviously a leader cannot please all his followers all the time, particularly when it comes to the allocation of scarce resources or necessary but unpopular chores. (It is a fortunate cricket captain who has eleven players who each prefer to occupy a different place in the batting order!) Even when it is possible to give everyone what they want, a good leader may decide that an alternative, and less popular, decision is in the best interests of the team. He will be wise to explain his rationale, so that his decision does not appear arbitrary and irrational. But it is his right to make his own decision, in his area of action responsibility; team members may feel that they would make a different decision if they were leader, but any expression of what this would entail can be treated merely as the voicing of a second opinion and ignored if desired.

Within this framework, the relationship between leader and team members becomes one of interdependence. Team members need a leader who does his job well, who provides them with the environment in which they can best get on with their own jobs effectively. A team leader is dependent for success on his team members doing their jobs well, because he is judged on their performance.

This is not a relationship of subservience; it is a relationship between equal human beings doing different jobs, one of which is the creation of a context in which the others can be successfully carried out. The person whose job this is might be perceived as more powerful than his colleagues, but his power is actually dependent on the performance of others. Looked at in this way his position can be seen as one of weakness!

It is only in quasi-military operational situations that instant obedience to a leader's instructions is required from team members. Even this cannot be called subservient behaviour if a contract has been entered into which explicitly demands it. Every cricketer knows that he must change his position on the field in response to his captain's signals – it is part of the game.

To carry this attitude into all business situations, however, is nonsense. 'I always do what my superior officer tells me,' said Walter, an ex-RAF wing commander colleague of mine, when doing something we both knew to be stupid. I am sure his boss would have liked to have had the opportunity to reconsider his decision in the light of the information Walter and I had. But Walter's unquestioning obedience deprived him of that opportunity.

We are right to resist the notion of followership; it has no place in the teamwork of the intelligent and autonomous. But a responsive and constructive attitude to leadership is an essential part of the role of team members.

'The first responsibility of a manager', according to Sir Nigel Foulkes, when he was Managing Director of Rank Xerox, 'is to educate his boss.' The same can be said of any team member in relation to his leader. A team member has first-hand knowledge and experience of what he is doing: his leader depends on *him* for his knowledge. A well-informed leader will make better decisions than an ignorant one.

Equally important is a team member's mentality, in particular the assumptions he makes concerning his leader. If he is suspicious and mistrustful, he interprets his leader's actions and decisions negatively, and his suspicions are reinforced – a case of self-justifying expectations. A willingness on the part of both the team members and the leader to give each other the benefit of the doubt – to 'assume positive intent' – is a good basis on which to build a secure relationship.

Team members must also be careful not to impose excessive expectations on their leader. He is as human as they are, and probably (hopefully?) on a learning curve too, so he is just as likely to make mistakes as they are. Tolerance of human fallibility, again extended by both parties, also helps in the building of understanding and trust between leader and team member.

The success of a relationship is indeed a mutual responsibility, a concept far removed from that of team members following their leader like sheep. The Leadership Trust use the term 'teammanship', and while this may be a little clumsy, it comes much closer to expressing what is appropriate than does 'followership'.

The leadership of the chief executive

The chief executive is the leader of the macro team, made up of many sub-teams and involving possibly thousands of people. He has special problems of leadership arising from the scale of the operation and the many channels and levels through which he must exert his influence.

He is also unique, as we have seen, in being alone; he is not a member of a higher level team with a leader to refer to for guidance and support. That might seem to be a blessing to a team member with an unsatisfactory boss, but it can leave the chief executive isolated. He is well-advised to seek the help of external advisers (corporate staff, consultants, non-executive directors, chief executives of other businesses, retired chief executives or simply wise friends) with whom he can share in confidence the problems he cannot, or chooses not to, discuss with his own immediate team.

He has a major communication problem, both in transmitting his message to the organization at large, and in keeping informed of what is happening. If he communicates down the hierarchy, there is a real danger that his message will be altered at each level as it is passed on. I have argued elsewhere* that the typical success rate in the average unstructured face-to-face communication is no higher than 25 per cent. Even if this is raised to 50 per cent by improved communication skills, the chances of success are down to 6 per cent after three transfers!

The setting up of briefing groups, which attend regularly scheduled meetings operating from a written brief, goes some way towards overcoming these problems, but in addition I believe a chief executive needs to communicate directly to all members of his organization periodically so that everyone knows where he intends the organization to go and how it should get there.

Probably the best way to do this is to address them directly at a series of meetings; if this is not feasible, a videotaped talk, with provision for everyone to see it, is probably the next best thing. A letter or newsletter is a poor substitute, because it loses the tone of voice and non-verbal dimensions of the message.

Everything a chief executive says and does is likely to be scrutinized for its significance by the organization. I suggest to chief

*See *Communication* in the Sphere 'Innovative Management Skills' series.

executives I work with that they imagine they are permanently plugged into a poor quality public address system. Everything they say comes over loud and indistinct or garbled.

The same principle applies to their actions, as one of them pointed out to me recently. He had just been appointed chief executive, and I phoned to congratulate him and arrange a meeting. He received the call warmly and then said, 'You weren't thinking of coming here, were you?' I was. 'Let's meet for dinner, instead,' he said. Over dinner he explained: 'If I were to be seen talking to you, all sorts of rumours and speculation would be flying round the organization before you left. They know what you stand for, and they would immediately draw their own conclusions – probably wrong ones. I don't want that happening.' Every action has to be assessed for its symbolic significance.

There is a similar problem with information coming up the organization. Of necessity it is summarized and filtered as it moves from one level to the next. In addition to the normal risk of faulty communication, there is the extra hazard of deliberate editing and window-dressing. No one wants to be the bearer of bad news; if it can be glossed over, it probably is, particularly if the prevailing management style is punitive. (One great advantage of a non-punitive style is that it increases the chances of accurate and honest reporting).

A chief executive, then, must supplement the formal information system with his own direct observation carried out on a sample basis, by 'walking the job' and talking to people at all levels in an informal, friendly way. He must make it clear that he is doing this for his own benefit, and to make himself known and visible in the organization. He must be scrupulously careful not to cut across the authority of sub-team leaders. When he encounters complaints (as is only inevitable) he should note them for future discussion with the managers concerned, in the course of which he will hear the rest of the story. (One chief executive of my acquaintance has an unfortunate habit of reacting with instant decisions to complaints he picks up on his walkabout, thereby infuriating and undermining the authority of the managers directly responsible, and making bad decisions at that. Any malcontent in the organization uses him when he wants to stir up trouble!)

The combination of a feel for the business as a whole and an ability to keep in touch with the nitty gritty, at least on a sample basis, is decribed by Dr Muller as the 'helicopter' quality, which he sees as the outstanding quality of a successful chief executive. It is a delicate combination which it takes considerable adroitness to maintain.

However, it is through his leadership of his own immediate team — the managers who report directly to him — that a chief executive sets the tone and direction of the business. Whatever messages he gives to the organization as a whole, they must be reinforced by the actions and behaviour of senior managers.

'You may think I have power, Vincent,' a chief executive said to me sadly, 'but I don't have power to change men's minds.' The chief executive is only as powerful as the team that supports him. If its members are not of one mind with him, either he or they must change, or he or they must go.

Leading for innovation

'If you love sausage and respect the law, do not be present when either is made.' This saying is quoted by George Prince in an unpublished paper, 'Managing Yourself for Innovation'. However desirable the end product — sausage, law or innovation — the *process* by which it is produced is messy and not for the squeamish. The innovation process is full of mistakes, anomalies and surprises.

For a team leader who wants his team to be innovative there is a serious dilemma. If he is a good manager, he is supposed to be in control of what his team does. Yet if he engages in controlling behaviour, he *inhibits* enterprise among his team members. 'Many of the actions and attitudes that are essential if subordinates are to maintain an innovative posture are for you, the manager, *counter intuitive* and *counter to your conservative training*. Counter, in fact, to many of the expectations transmitted to you by your boss. Yet failing to recognize and be in synch with the innovative process of subordinates sends a loud clear signal to stay mundane and keep you comfortable.'*

One solution for a team leader is not to look too closely — to exercise the Nelson touch, you might say, and to do so in both directions, down as well as up the organization! (In other words, don't be present when the sausage is made.) Alternatively, as George puts it, 'Shield your boss, and to some extent yourself, from the messier aspects of innovation.' It is an uncomfortable notion for me — it suggests almost an abdication of leadership — yet I find myself increasingly behaving in this way, and lo, innovation is flourishing in my team!

Ideally, a team leader and his team (and his boss!) need a

*George Prince, ibid.

common understanding of the innovation process, so that he can behave, and be perceived to be behaving, in a manner appropriate to the current stage of the process being carried out at any particular time – permissive and supportive in the experimental stages, hard-nosed and controlling when far-reaching, high-risk decisions have to be taken.

The innovation process is an iterative cycle, progressing from speculative thought which generates new ways of dealing with a problem or opportunity, to specific actionable ideas that can be tested in some form of pilot scheme or experiment. An experiment provides data, which may prompt fresh directions of thought and new ideas which are in turn subjected to test, until an idea is solid enough to be implemented as a solution. A leader and his team members need a common understanding of this process, and to be in agreement as to what stage they are at with any particular innovation, so that they think and behave in the appropriate way at all times.

The duty of a leader in promoting innovation in his team is to create an environment which encourages innovation, rather than do all or most of the innovating himself. Although one of the ways he can create such an environment is to set an example of innovative behaviour by taking on new challenges himself, thereby encouraging others to do likewise, the area within which he does this must not take in those tasks properly carried out by his team members, only those which it is his responsibility as leader to attend to.

To stimulate innovation in the area of team tasks, he needs to find 'champions' from within his team. If he sees an opportunity for innovation, he must offer it to a team member on the understanding that he is free to tackle it in his own way and should not feel compelled to employ methods which he himself would choose. A leader's own ideas and opinions should be offered as a resource to the champion: whether he adopts them or not is up to him.

A champion should check with his leader before taking any action that might represent an encroachment on his leader's area of action responsibility, i.e. action which might put substantial team resources or the team's reputation at risk. If a proposal is not acceptable to a leader, he must give feedback in a constructive way: 'These aspects are acceptable and these are the problems we need to overcome before going ahead.' *How* problems are overcome is for the champion to decide (and remains subject to his leader's approval). Again, his leader's own ideas are available to him, if he wants them.

By delegating opportunities for innovation to team members, and by encouraging team members to come up with their own proposals for innovation, a leader mobilizes the innovative capacity of his whole team — a much more effective approach than attempting to do all the jobs himself. Innovative activity is usually the most interesting, stimulating and exciting part of a job, and carries the highest potential for learning. Ideally, all team members should have some share in it.

It is equally a part of a leader's job to keep innovative activity in balance with the routine work of his team. Businesses succeed in the short term through the efficient implementation of well-tried, solutions; they survive and grow over the long term through the process of innovation. Neither activity must crowd out the other; each has its proper place and calls for its appropriate style of working. It is a leader's responsibility to create an environment in which a suitable degree of innovation co-exists with the efficient performance of routine operations.

5. Team composition and formation

Introduction

How do you put together a group of people who will work well as a team? Or, given an existing group, how do you arrange the mix (assuming you have some power to do so) to ensure the maximum chance of it becoming a successful team? Given that some highly successful teams come together spontaneously, is it possible to emulate that phenomenon through the conscious choice of team members?

There are no guarantees, but I believe you can weight the odds in your favour by selecting a mix that is both complementary and compatible. To the extent that these two partly contradictory characteristics co-exist, you have a team that is functionally effective (assuming, of course, that the individuals concerned are sufficiently technically competent to carry out their jobs). What cannot be guaranteed is that they actually *like* each other; to the extent that they *dis*like each other, you carry a potential for the development of seriously disruptive emotional problems in the team.

There exists a variety of approaches to the systematic selection of people who will form a balanced, complementary whole. They all start from a recognition that people differ in their aptitudes for and in their desire to undertake a given activity. If individuals' aptitudes and desires are identified and matched with the requirements of a team, the best of all worlds is had — round pegs in round holes, all the necessary holes filled, and the individuals blending into a harmonious, mutually supportive whole.

Differences in approach arise over how the aptitudes and desires of individuals are described and measured, and how they are translated into roles in a team. Certain psychometric tests are applied in the interpretation of individuals in terms of 'personality factors'; other methods are employed to describe people in terms of the team roles to which they appear most suited.

In my experience, there is one approach that is unique in its key methodology for the assessment of individual aptitudes. This is the method of Action Profile developed by Warren Lamb, Pamela Ramsden and their associates in Action Profile International. It is based on observations of elements of non-verbal behaviour in an individual, whereas all the other approaches rely on verbal data, either gathered by means of questionnaires or recorded during group discussions.

Non-verbal behaviour strikes me as a source of uniquely reliable data. It is involuntary and cannot be faked. Through it, a person exhibits a constant mix of behavioural elements, be he acting or drunk. A questionnaire can be invalidated by false replies (though a well-designed questionnaire does have internal checks for consistency).

The use of non-verbal data also accords with our intuitive approach to forming impressions and making judgements about people. Many of the adjectives we use to describe people relate to physical aspects — 'deliberate', 'ponderous', 'agile', 'quick', 'alert'. It would be unheard of to hire someone without meeting them. We can get verbal information through correspondence and phone conversations, but we know we have to meet a person to find out what he or she is *really* like. When we meet someone the impressions we form of them are stimulated by our experience of their non-verbal behaviour. This process can only take place when people are face to face with one another, hence the knowledge that it is essential to meet a candidate for a job before deciding on his or her suitability. Action Profile performs the same task of recording and analysing non-verbal behaviour in a systematic and disciplined way.

I have used Action Profile as a tool in team formation and analysis for over a quarter of a century and have found it invaluable. I propose to discuss my experience in depth, with little reference to other methods (of which I have no experience as a user).

The disadvantage of Action Profile is that it needs a trained practitioner to make the observations and is therefore more expensive than questionnaire-based systems. However, given the importance of the issues at stake and the cost of a wrong decision, the differences in cost seem to me to be unimportant. In this field, it pays to buy the best quality without regard to relatively minor differences in price!

Action profiles

The following description of action profiles is based on material supplied by Eddie Bows, one of the principal UK practitioners. Fuller treatment can be found in *Top Team Planning*, by Pamela Ramsden; *Management Behaviour*, by Warren Lamb and David Turner; and *Body Code: The Meaning in Movement*, by Warren Lamb and Elizabeth Watson. The best simple introduction is *Executives in Action*, by Carol-Lynne Moore.

Action profiling, unlike many other assessment techniques, is unique in its methodology. Unlike those techniques which rely on the answering of questions and the ticking of boxes, some of which can be applied by a subject to him- or herself, action profiling is carried out entirely independently of a subject's conscious behaviour. Comparisons with the 16 PF, Costic, Miers Briggs and other tests are meaningless because an action profile is concerned with that aspect of motivation which is believed not to change significantly over time under normal circumstances. (Abnormal circumstances are constituted by, for example a nervous breakdown or some form of brainwashing — in fact, any experience sufficient to induce a significant change in personality.)

In action profiling the assessment of motivation is based entirely on information which the subject provides unconsciously. It is entirely non-verbal in origin. It is not, however, what is commonly referred to as 'body language'. Body language, which has many interesting applications, is to do with those aspects of non-verbal communication which are usually transitory and which may be used in role play or to create a particular impression.

Action profiling relies on the analysis of a highly specialized form of non-verbal behaviour, described by Warren Lamb (the pioneer of the technique) as 'integrated movement'. Every individual has a particular repertoire of integrated movement which has been shown to reflect his or her unique way of thinking about decisions and problems and the way this thinking is perceived by those with whom he or she comes into contact. *Integrated movement cannot be faked.* A subject cannot influence his or her action profile through any conscious effort.

Action profiling is essentially a technique which describes the way people prefer to make decisions, solve problems, drive cars, buy houses and do whatever else requires a degree of initiative. An action profile is, in fact, a measure of intrinsic motivation. It is not in any way a measure of ability, skill, intelligence, experience, education or, indeed, anything else.

Consider decision making as a three stage process, as follows:

(a) *Attending* e.g. giving attention to the situation, defining what you mean, surveying, analysing, researching;
(b) *Intending* e.g. forming an intention to go ahead, making a case for what you want to do, building resolve, making the issues clear, weighing up the pros and cons;
(c) *Committing* e.g. committing yourself to action, progressing your decisions, seizing opportunities, timing and staging your actions.

Most of us like to believe that our decisions are balanced in some way, that they reflect pertinent research and thorough preparation, are purposeful and realistic, and are implemented at the right time and according to a plan. In action profile terms, a sound decision reflects a balance between attending, intending and committing, appropriate to the context in which it is made.

We can all think of situations in which so-and-so 'didn't do his homework', 'gave up too easily' or 'missed the boat'. Such situations reflect particular motivational imbalances between the three action profile stages. The first suggests a low attending motivation, the second a low intending motivation and the third a low committing motivation. We can just as well think of situations in which a high attending, intending or committing motivation applies. For example, someone who is a stickler for detail has a high attending motivation, and so on.

In action profiling, the three stages of decision-making together carry a total score of 100 per cent. Each stage is divided into two individual action motivations, as follows:

Attending – investigating (analysing, establishing method);
     – exploring (looking for new ideas and alternatives);
Intending – determining (persisting against difficult odds);
     – evaluating (weighing up the pros and cons);
Committing – timing (taking the opportunity);
     – anticipating (having objectives, planning ahead).

A score for one of these six action motivations of 20 per cent or more indicates high motivation in that area. Any score below 10 per cent indicates low motivation. Theoretically, an ideal balance is represented by six scores of 16⅔ per cent. In reality, the most effective teams seem to be those which consist of people with both high and low individual motivations, but which carry an average score of around 16 per cent for each motivation.

Clearly, the most appropriate balance for a particular team, company or situation depends on the context and the environment in which decisions are taken. According to Eddie Bows there are three main types of situation represented by strength in each of the three stages of decision-making. Taken in turn these are as follows:

Attending Strength in this area is most appropriate when a company is breaking new ground and the environment is constantly changing.

Intending Strength in this area is of most value when a company has reached rock bottom and it is essential that considerable strength, determination and realism be brought to bear in order to pull the company round.

Committing Strength in this area is needed when a company's main concern is to be competitive and to stay ahead of the competition.

It follows that since all chief executives have action profiles, some conclusions can be reached about their particular styles of decision-making. They may, of course, have balanced action profiles but this is very unusual. They are much more likely to have profiles or decision-making styles which reflect strength in some areas and weaknesses in others. Those who are really successful seem to have an intuitive feel for those of their colleagues who are strong where they are weak. They are also able to modify actual behaviour for short periods to meet the needs of a particular situation.

An action profile provides a framework in which a chief executive can consider his own style and the style of his colleagues. It shows him at a glance who can support him in his weaker areas and, equally importantly, it highlights the areas in which each subordinate needs support.

An action profile also describes 'interaction motivation' – the way a person's action motivation is perceived and experienced by those around him. It reflects the extent to which others are invited to share in, or to be excluded from, his or her attending, intending and committing processes. The sharer generates an environment in which colleagues are consulted about decisions being taken. The private interactor prefers independence and generates a more autocratic style of management. Some people are versatile, in the sense of being able to include or exclude others as they wish. Others are neutral – their willingness to interact exists but needs to be activated by another's initiative.

A high motivation is not necesarily a strength or a low motivation a weakness; there are positive and negative aspects of both a high and a low motivation. People have a tendency to over-indulge the activities for which they have a high motivation. This is only natural, because these are the kinds of activity with which they are most comfortable, but it may not be appropriate to a particular situation in hand.

Conversely, a low motivation provides a freedom from the need to spend much time and energy on an activity, and in some situations this can be an advantage. There is no such thing as a 'perfect' profile; a profile is more or less appropriate for a job, which means that an individual tends to do a job in a particular, individual way.

For example, my own strongest motivation is in evaluating (weighing up pros and cons), which is great for deciding between strategies, policies and priorities. The downside is a tendency to pre-judge and rule out options because they seem to be impracticable or otherwise unsuitable. I have a colleague who has a particularly low score in the same area. For him all options merit serious consideration: quite often he attempts a course of action that I would judge quite unfeasible – and succeeds!

Such a difference indicates enormous potential for synergy in a team – and an equally enormous potential for disruption. On the positive side, my colleague can open my mind to possibilities that I tend to ignore if left to myself; I can learn from his achievements that more opportunities for action exist than I generally take into account. In addition, owing to my powers of evaluation, I can provide him with assistance in ordering his priorities. He can then use his energies in a discriminating fashion, pursuing those opportunities most likely to bring success or deliver the highest payoff.

For this synergy to work, we need to understand one another's very different ways of working and appreciate the value of each other's approach. Our action profiles provide us with sufficient data, and a common language, to identify our differences and to work out how best to use our combined strengths to our mutual benefit.

Without this data, it is all too easy for me to consider my colleague undiscriminating and irresponsible and for him to dismiss me as restrictive and controlling. (Even with the data we still have our problems! But at least we know what is causing them, which makes them easier to deal with.)

When the action profiles of all of a team's members have been prepared, a comprehensive team analysis and report is presented to the team leader in preparation for a joint meeting or seminar with the entire team. The report describes the current balance or imbalance which exists individually or collectively and makes recommendations according to the context in which the team operates. The context might embrace such elements as the company's organizational structure, its standing in the market, its products, its profitability or its diversification programme. A particular motivational balance is neither good nor bad in itself. It is simply more or less appropriate to the circumstances prevailing.

The seminar is used to provide each team member with a new perspective on the decision-making styles of his colleagues and how these styles relate to his own. Each member is viewed as a dynamic part of a whole. He can influence others and be influenced by them. For the first time, perhaps, he is given a structure in which to proffer influence. More importantly, he knows when and under what circumstances he should seek the influence of a colleague with a strength in his own weaker motivational areas.

Selecting people to fill vacancies in teams can be a problem because there are often two potentially conflicting forces at work. On the one hand, an attempt is made to improve the balance of an existing team by bringing in someone new to the organization. The intention here is not necessarily to create balance such that the six average scores of the team are roughly equal. It may be deliberately to create a certain type of imbalance in order to fill a particular need, e.g. to introduce a higher level of committing to bolster up the company's selling activities.

On the other hand, a vacant position may require someone with a profile strong in certain areas of motivation, but whose appointment, precisely on account of his or her particular strengths, would produce an undesirable imbalance within the team.

That either the filling of a team's particular functional needs or the maintaining of an otherwise desirable balance within a team be to an extent compromised is often inevitable, but the decision as to which of these should suffer can be taken before an appointment is made. Whichever view prevails, it is possible to exercise control before, rather than after, the event.

It is clearly possibly to plan 'ideal' teams using action profiles. Some companies use them for precisely this purpose. Mr Ian Marks, Managing Director of Trebor, was quoted in the *Financial Times* are saying he used action profiling to 'balance continually' his management team.

A team leader must be prepared to allow his subordinates' motivational strengths to make good his own weakneses. For example, a chief executive may recognize his weakness in, say, exploring, a deficiency which makes his approach to decision-making rather narrow. Despite his recognition of the problem, however, the motivational urge not to adapt to new ideas is overriding. Experience suggests that the most effective way to compensate for such a weakness is to employ a highly motivated 'explorer' to provide new ideas and to encourage lateral thinking. This releases the chief executive to be himself while recognizing and using the strengths of his colleagues.

At a more philosophical level, I believe it is essential to appreciate that different individuals achieve their results in quite different ways, and that those ways are 'right' for them. There is no one right way. I see many managers (especially successful ones) operating on the unconscious assumption that there is one right way – the way they do things themselves! It's understandable, because that way has been successful for them, but it cuts them off from appreciating and using the potential of people with different ways of achieving results.

I have found action profiles very valuable as a means of creating awareness of different styles of working. They encourage tolerance of differences and ultimately a willingness to seek help from colleagues with high motivations in areas where one's own are low.

Applications of Action Profile

The data from an action profile can be used in several ways:

— to fit an individual to a job (and vice versa!);
— to inform team members of their own and their colleagues' preferred working styles;

— to build balanced teams;

— to identify areas in which an individual or a team need to be supplemented by systems, structures or external support by way of compensation for a bias or weakness in profile.

Fitting an individual to a job. The most obvious application is to recruitment, but equally important are transfers and other changes in team composition. In principle, it should be possible to specify, in broad outline at least, the action profile required for a particular job, as a guide to recruitment. Maybe a market researcher or a research scientist should have a high attending motivation, a salesman a high committing and sharing motivation, etc.

Unfortunately jobs are not as simple as that, and job titles can be misleading about the job content. A corporate planner, for example, does not 'plan' – his job is to devise planning systems and to ensure that the managers in an organization produce plans according to a format and timetable which allow him to combine them in a single corporate plan. A research and development director is unlikely to engage in either research and development (though he should probably have experience in both).

To the best of my knowledge, no systematic research has yet been carried out to identify the action profiles of the people who are most successful in different types of job. Intuitively, I would expect there to be some clear correlations between motivations and successful performance, but it is by no means certain, because people in the same kind of work may achieve success in quite different ways.

An action profile can demonstrate that performance in a job can be drastically affected not by the job itself, but by the way the individual is asked to work. A dramatic case, from my own experience, was Richard, a young OR analyst, who was hired by his previous boss, Alan, when Alan came to work for me, because Richard's experience exactly fitted a field of work we were developing.

After a few months, Alan said to me, 'I think I've made a mistake in hiring Richard. I put him straight into Project X because I knew he had experience of that sort of work, and he made a mess of it. So I switched him to Project Y, which he should have been able to take in his stride, and he's made a mess of that. Either he's not the man I thought he was, or we're doing something wrong.'

We decided, with Richard's agreement, to have his action profile assessed. The profiler (Warren Lamb) told us: 'Richard is the kind of person who needs always to start at the beginning. If you pitch him into something ongoing in midstream, he will try to fight his way back to the source before he can contribute effectively.'

'So I've been using him in exactly the wrong way,' said Alan, 'pitching him into projects that were already in progress.' He took him off Project Y and gave him Project A to start up. Richard did so with conspicuous success; when I bumped into him twelve years later, he was still working happily for the company, long after Alan and I had left. (Today, incidentally, I would not normally hire someone without seeing their action profile first.)

Team understanding: When all the action profiles of a team's members have been prepared and dicussed with the individuals, so that each person has a good understanding of his own profile, the results are usually presented to the team as a whole. Team members can relate their experience of working with colleagues to their own and their colleagues' profiles.

Problems in working relationships can often be explained in terms of differences in profile. A high attender would probably see a high committer as impetuous – he would seem to be taking action without giving due attention to finding out the facts and exploring the options. ('Due attention' for a high attender is the amount of attention *he* wants to give it – a lot!) Conversely, a high committer would find a high attender dilatory, perhaps theoretical, and reluctant to get on with the action.

Similarly, a high intender can be perceived as resolute; equally, the same characteristic can be experienced as stubbornness or bossiness. These are all judgemental and emotive terms which are unlikely to be helpful in discussing relationships.

Action profiles provide a neutral, factual basis for discussing the different styles of different people, and the likely interaction between them. People who are having difficulties can discuss them in the common language of Action Profile while sharing an understanding of each other's preferred style of operation.

The same information can be used in deciding what type of activity (in action profile terms) is demanded by a situation and in making a conscious decision to get into that mode of operation. Firefighting in a crisis, for example, needs everyone working in the committing mode; high attenders and intenders know they must switch out of their preferred mode into committing. Developing a strategy is more a matter for the attending mode – committers need to curb their impatience. These are differences in degree of course, and most people can operate successfully in their areas of low motivation for short periods when they know that is required of them.

We have found, in fact, that many people can 'flex' their profiles when asked to. At a meeting at which roles and responsibilities are clearly defined and an explicit structure is imposed (like a Synectics meeting), each individual knows what kind of contribution is expected from him at each stage of the meeting. Under these conditions, and for relatively short periods of time, it seems that most people can behave in ways that are not typical of their profile. This is an important quality and enables a team of diverse personalities to pull together.

Perhaps the greatest single benefit accruing to a team from the use of action profiles is a marked increase in the level of mutual tolerance and appreciation. Without realizing they are doing so, many people act on the assumption that 'the person whose decision-making process is different from mine is wrong, i.e. those who think as I do are right and those who think differently are wrong'.*

Action profilers stand that assumption on its head: it becomes 'because our decision-making processes are different, we are in a position to enrich each other should we feel this desirable; he represents a valuable resource to me, as I do to him, and provided we get our act together we can both benefit.' 'Getting our act together', in this context, is a matter of recognizing which dimensions of an action profile are appropriate to the task in hand, and working through them one at a time.

In this way the irritation and even contempt that can easily be experienced as a result of a colleague's very different way of working can be replaced by understanding and appreciation – a big step forward in internal team relationships.

Building a balanced team: One of the great temptations for a manager is to recruit in his own image – if I believe I am a capable person, people like me must also be capable, so I hire people like me! Usually it is not a conscious or explicit policy; it tends to be followed unconsciously through the selection criteria that are applied.

The result is likely to be a skewed or biased team, with most members showing the same predominant characteristics. Such a team tends to get along well, but tends also to be rather unsuccessful. Team members become puzzled by their lack of success, because they are proud of their teamwork (they are great friends, socially as well as at work). In fact, they are a great club, but a poor team.

A team like this lacks some essential dimension – it doesn't fire on

*Carole Lynne Moore, *Executives in Action*, Macdonald and Evans, 1982.

all six cylinders of the action profile! Moreover, any individual who is brought in to provide the missing elements has the greatest difficulty fitting in. He is perceived as an outsider, a maverick, not 'one of us', and tends to find his contribution rejected. He, too, ends up feeling frustrated and rejected and probably leaves even before he is asked to!

A well-balanced team, in action profile terms, is one in which the average score for each of the six motivations lies between 12 per cent and 20 per cent. (I think it is pedantic and unrealistic to try to get close to the theoretical ideal of 16⅔ per cent for each quality.) Usually the effect of a new recruit on team balance is unlikely to be so critical as to determine whether or not he should be hired; it is generally sufficient to be aware of his effect on the team mix.

However, I have on three occasions made recruitment decisions almost entirely on the basis of the effect on the team profile. One was negative – I turned down a well-qualified, experienced and likeable candidate solely because his profile compounded an existing bias in the team. (Fortunately, he was also an action profile user, and understood the reason for the decision!) It is impossible to know whether it was a good decision or not, but neither of us has had reason to regret it since.

In the other cases, my colleagues and I set out deliberately to fill a deficiency in our team profile. In each case, the best candidate in action profile terms turned out to be someone without relevant qualifications or experience for the job. Taking a deep breath, we went ahead and hired the individuals on the basis that the jobs could be learned but that action profiles could not! Their respective appointments have turned out (after stressful learning periods) to have been entirely justified. Both the individuals and the team have benefited.

Going for a balanced team creates its own problems in terms of interpersonal relationships. Just as a biased team tends naturally to be a cosy group which gets along, so a balanced team has built into it the seeds of conflict because of the diversity of natural styles.

To some extent, understanding each other's profile reduces the problem, individuals coming to see colleagues' different ways of working as a resource which can supplement and complement their own. (As a low anticipator, I find it great to work with someone who orders tomorrow morning's taxi the night before – it does not normally occur to me to do such a thing!)

At the rational level, such mutual understanding works well, though it does call for an investment by everyone concerned in learning what profiles mean. However, in my experience, it does not seem to be sufficient to deal with deep-seated emotional difficulties between team members (neither, incidentally, is anything else that I know of!)

I have at times wondered whether deliberately building a biased team and finding other ways to compensate for missing qualities might make life simpler by reducing the potential for emotional problems in the team. So far I have not needed to experiment in this direction, but ways in which an individual and a team can compensate for missing qualities are discussed below.

Complementing the action profile: The information from an action profile identifies areas where an individual or a team is vulnerable because of low motivation. While it seems unlikely than an individual profile can be changed (and possibly undesirable to attempt to do so), there are a number of ways in which support can be provided to minimize risk.

A profile itself creates awareness that a problem or need exists, an essential first step. People who lack a particular motivation tend to be unaware that such a thing exists, and therefore do not realize that they lack it! (They may find that information from a profile explains problems they have experienced; for example, when I discovered that I was a low anticipator it explained my tendency to be late for appointments and miss planes and trains!)

One way to compensate is to provide colleagues with the missing qualities, i.e. build a balanced team, but this is not always possible, and there is no guarantee that a complementary colleague will always be available to help. A team as a whole has to operate with some degree of imbalance, and it is important to have means of supplementing areas of weakness.

For both an individual and a team, training in the techniques of providing assistance in weak areas is worth trying. (For my low anticipating, a time management system is an obvious aid, like spectacles for the short sighted!) Note that this is a different *kind* of training from that which an individual spontaneously opts for. He usually wants to learn more about the things that interest him, and these generally lie in the area of his strongest motivation. Consequently, training tends to reinforce his strengths and do nothing for his weaknesses.

Equally, an individual struggles with the compensating kind of course. (I did a time management course, did not enjoy it much, and even now do not make much use of the techniques I was taught, even though I know they are 'good for me'!) Even so, the effort is worth making. Equally valuable are any disciplines or routines an individual can develop for himself – today, I work out a timetable for myself in order to ensure I get to the airport on time and no longer miss planes!

In the case of a team imbalance, it is helpful to employ external specialists in areas of weakness as both consultants and trainers. A good example is given by Carole-Lynne Moore.* A team she describes as The Achievers had a management of individuals recognized as outstanding talents in their fields but were not meshing as a functional team. The team action profile showed a 34:66 imbalance between the 'perspective' components (exploring, evaluating and anticipating) and the 'effort' components (investigating, determining and timing). 'This meant that although the team tended to be aggressive in its actions, decisions were made without a sense of what the company mission was, or what the long range implications and results of a decision would be.'†

Their solution was to use a consultant in strategic management (an individual with high perspective motivations) to run a series of seminars on strategy formulation. As well as successfully developing a strategy for the company (thereby filling an important vacuum), the exercise enhanced the team's understanding of their individual collective profiles, on the strength of which they drew up a set of operating guidelines in order to capitalize on their strengths and safeguard them where they were vulnerable.

In this particular case, the group not only hired an outside consultant to supply missing elements in their profile; they also made a massive commitment in terms of time and energy to working in an area (strategy development) in which they had little spontaneous interest. This willingness to work against the grain of its natural inclinations is required of any group which wants to compensate for low levels of motivation in any area.

Another method of compensating for low levels is to use a 'horses for courses' approach to particular tasks, even when this might cut across normal functional responsibilities. In the case described above, the production director was given responsibility for a new products project, because he was the highest anticipator in the group. The marketing director, to whom it would be assigned conventionally, was quite happy to pass the responsibility to a colleague who was temperamentally more suited to it.

*op. cit., pp. 115–21.
†ibid.

Other assessment methods

I have concentrated on the use of action profiles because this is the area in which I have experience, as well as confidence in the basic assessment technique. In principle, alternative assessment methods should yield many of the same benefits, namely:

— the ability to build a balanced team;
— awareness and understanding of individuals' different ways of achieving results (an increase in the level of mutual tolerance);
— 'horses for courses', in the sense of fitting an individual to a job and using the most suitable individual for a particular task;
— compensation in known areas of team and individual weakness;
— provision of a common language in which people can discuss their own and their colleagues' styles of working.

My impression, however, is that most psychometric techniques focus on the development of the individual rather than on team development, although there is one approach, the Margerison–McCann Team Management Index, that is geared specifically to the composition and operation of teams. This index is calculated using a self-completion questionnaire, of sixty items which takes about ten or fifteen minutes to finish.

A completed questionnaire is used to produce a detailed personal profile covering a number of key areas fundamental to the work process. These include:

— team role overview
— work preferences
— interpersonal relationships
— decision making
— team building
— leadership preferences
— self organization
— information management
— personal profiling summary'*

(A lot to ask of such a short questionnaire, you may think!)
A profile thus derived is related to the following classification of work functions involved in team management:

*Charles Margerison and Dick McCann, *How to Lead a Winning Team*, MCB University Press, 1985.

- Advising
- Innovating
- Promoting
- Developing
- Organizing
- Producing
- Inspecting
- Maintaining

The first four are described as diverging activities and the second four converging, corresponding to the traditional staff and line distinction in management theory. There is also a ninth function, Linking, which co-ordinates and integrates all the others and also deals with relationships with units outside a team.

The authors go on to apply a behavioural label to each of the functions, coming up with role descriptions such as 'thruster organizer', 'creator innovator', etc. Classification of an individual under one of these headings provides his 'major profile'.

I have not used this approach myself, so I cannot comment on it from experience. I believe any system that encourages members of a team to understand their own and each other's preferred mode of working is of value. Discussion of the key areas and work functions is likely to have a sort of Hawthorn effect, by making participants aware of the issues, emphasizing the existence and value of diversity and developing a common language for yet further discussion of team working styles.

I am, however, suspicious of the tendency to classify people in convenient boxes, and of the apparently arbitrary allocation of behavioural labels to these boxes. (The urge to classify seems to be a characteristic of academics!) I am also concerned that the basic data used are 'work preferences' as expressed in the answers on the questionnaire. People have preferences based on their own experience, but they may not have experience of situations likely to bring out the full range of their capabilities. And I am not sure that my preferences are for what I am best at – a lot of clowns want to play Hamlet!

6. Training for teamwork and leadership

Introduction

If the quality of teamwork and team leadership is critical to the performance of an organization – and personally I believe it is more critical than any other single factor over the long term – it makes sense to work at developing it to the highest possible degree. Investment in team training and other team development events becomes a high priority, particularly for an organization seeking to achieve significant change in its style, culture and performance.

There is inevitably a plethora of approaches available in the market place. A useful booklet published by the Coverdale Organization* summarizes, in its 1979 edition, no fewer than twenty-five different selected approaches; anyone who wanted to could no doubt come up with a further twenty-five today.

I do not propose to offer any kind of comprehensive review of the field, still less attempt an assessment of those which represent the 'best buy'. Not only am I not qualified to do so, I am positively disqualified by being an active practitioner in the field with a strong bias in favour of the type of training my own company provides! The following exposition is therefore limited to those activities of which I have some knowledge and which I believe have something useful to offer.

There is a sense in which any time a team takes to examine, reflect on and improve its methods of working together is bound to be beneficial. The mere fact of stopping to think, in the hurly-burly of everyday activity, is as valuable for a team as it is for an individual.

*Susan Scott (ed.), *Behavioural Theories*, 2nd edn, Coverdale Organization, 1979.

Being together for an extended period of time (typically three to five days) gives team members a chance to get to know one another as people (although it does not guarantee that they will like each other any better!)

Sharing an experience that is different from those typically undergone every day has a bonding effect, even when (perhaps particularly when!) it is a bad one. It becomes a common reference point, maybe a shared and exclusive joke. Moreover, people who are good at learning from experience learn from *any* new experience, which is why the better courses wisely put a lot of emphasis on the conscious learning process itself.

I believe it is essential for teams regularly (once or twice a year) to take time off to take stock of how they are working and how they can improve their ways of operating. Whether this should take the form of a training course, or some other kind of event – a workshop or conference, for example – depends on a team's circumstances.

The benefit to be had from going through a team training process *first* is that it provides some commonly agreed processes and structures, and a common language, which the team can use subsequently, with or without external help.

The time spent is costly in terms of executive hours, quite apart from trainers' fees and residential expenses. If an overhead ratio of 150 per cent is applied, the cost for a £20,000-a-year executive works out at about £1,000 a week (allowing for holidays). It is, proportionately more expensive for higher paid executives. A five day course, then, 'costs' £8,000 for a group of eight before it starts! Alternatively, the expense can be viewed as a straight 'opportunity cost' – think of the value of the work the executives would be doing if they were not on the course (which *ought* to come out at an even higher figure!)

How can you tell whether a course has been worth the time and money invested in it? I know of no other criterion than the judgement of the participants, both at the end of the course and some time later, say three to six months. However, it has the weakness of being entirely subjective, and 'contaminated' by the relationship the trainer will have developed with individual participants – he may even have brainwashed them! There is also, I suspect, a compulsion on the part of course attenders to justify the time they have spent ('I've spent a week doing this. It must have been worthwhile.')!

A more objective measure would be team performance, before and after the course, but this is likely to be affected by many external variables as well. If it were possible to isolate performance in one or two co-operative areas — the efficiency and productiveness of management meetings, for example — we might have a reasonably objective and relevant criterion.

An organization which regularly conducts attitude surveys has an overall measure of the changes effected by training along with whatever other initiatives have taken place over the same time. Again, it is difficult to isolate the training effect. Feedback from 'customers' of the trained group, i.e. the people who have a regular interface with them, is much more specific if obtainable.

For example, the marketing department of a company came to Synectics for training because they had observed the change in the design department we had trained. They had become much easier to work with and more constructive. In the same way, another marketing department decided to take the Synectics course because they had seen the effect of our training on their advertising agency. (I have also to confess that sometimes we have people on our courses who say, 'This would really benefit my boss', and we have to admit that his boss received the same training some time previously!)

In the following sections, I want to explore some of the issues surrounding training in more depth and in the context of three specific types of training:

— Coverdale Training
— The Synectics Innovative Teamwork Programme
— Adventure Training, conducted by the Leadership Trust and others

Coverdale Training

Coverdale Training probably represents the most popular and widely adopted approach to team training in the UK over the last twenty years. It was originally developed by the late Ralph Coverdale within Esso and became an independent company in 1966.

Coverdale's teaching formula provides a structure within which there is freedom for ideas to develop over the years.

The underlying philosophy is that 'in industry and business, the emphasis must ultimately be on getting things done'. The two-fold aim is 'to enable people to learn from experience and develop skills which are relevant to co-operating with others in getting things done'. Practical activities provide a vehicle for both kinds of learning.

A course is based on practical activity. From the very start, clients are involved in a series of short activities which involve them mentally and physically. The physical involvement is not military-styled physical exercise, rather the performing of unusual mental tasks in public.

Tutors set tasks according to the emerging needs of clients and conclusions reached in the frequent review discussions. Printed summaries of the house-message are given after these reviews, but they are considered to be no more authoritative than the personal notes of those taking part.

Courses are hotel-based and much of their spirit is generated by the need for each course to create its own environment. Tasks may be simple and short, even silly and frantic. As indicated above, individuals are sometimes required to go into town to do unusual things – carry out interviews, undertake research, etc.

In order to develop the ability to learn from experience, Coverdale stresses the sequence of Plan, Do, Review (as does the Synectics course). Planning involves specifying the aims of an activity, recognizing that several aims may be involved at once and that they may be individual or shared. It also involves specifying criteria of success in specific measurable terms, in order that the question 'How will we know whether we have been successful?' can be answered.

Course participants are trained to observe the process of what is happening, i.e. *how* things are being done, as opposed to what the task is – to develop an awareness of the kinds of activity that contribute to success or failure in the attempt to achieve objectives. Observation is the necessary means of providing data for review meetings, out of which the learning is drawn for the next experiment.

Co-operative skills are developed by encouraging supportive behaviour such as listening, building on ideas and putting forward creative proposals, and deliberate planning for co-operation.

In summary, the themes running through Coverdale training can be described as follows:

— use of the naturally occurring stages of thought and action in an orderly sequence – a systematic approach to getting things done and achieving objectives;
— identification and co-ordination of purpose, success criteria and objectives;
— gaining people's commitment to their work, their team and their organization;

— setting measures of success and self-monitoring of performance;
— overall awareness – observation – necessary for the implementation of improvements appropriate to a situation;
— recognition and use of personal strengths and skills;
— listening, building on ideas and making creative proposals;
— deliberate planning for co-operation;
— responsive use of authority appropriate to the demands of a situation;
— trial and success learning.

It could be argued that all the above are matters of common sense and do not need a training course to inculcate them. I disagree. If you observe people at work you will find that the principles represented above are ignored more often than not. 'Common sense' is not common practice!

My own experience of working with Coverdale trained people is that they are significantly more receptive to the methods I want to introduce than those who have not had training of this kind. They already have an awareness of process and the need for positive and supportive behaviour. They take readily to additional techniques and structures that increase the probability of constructive behaviour.

My one reservation about Coverdale Training is a suspicion that it might encourage the avoidance of conflict rather than its resolution. People are so concerned to be nice to one another that they sweep disagreements under the carpet rather than rock the boat. I remember observing a meeting in a Coverdale trained organization (and Coverdale insist that *all* members in an organization should be trained) in which every time a topic looked like becoming controversial, the chairman said, to the agreement of all present, 'I think we should deal with this outside the meeting.' It was an organization with many unresolved but submerged conflicts.

It may be unfair to attribute this characteristic to Coverdale Training; it may well have existed in the organization long beforehand. Coverdale, however, had certainly not dislodged it, and there is, too, a very English quality to the Coverdale approach that is consistent with the view that it is not gentlemanly to disagree, at least in public! I prefer the more direct and open American approach, which brings conflict out in the open. It can then be resolved, provided the skills exist to do so constructively. Unskilled attempts to resolve conflict can, of course, be destructive, although no more so than leaving it to fester underground.

The Synectics Innovative Teamwork Programme

The Synectics Innovative Teamwork Programme (ITP) shares with Coverdale the focus on process awareness, the systematic approach of Plan, Do, Review, and the necessity for constructive feedback and good listening and supportive behaviour. It differs in its emphasis on the innovative dimension, through the development of creative problem-solving skills. It also focusses attention on the unique responsibility of each member of a team through the concept of action responsibility (see Chapter 2). The combination of creative problem-solving skills and the action responsibility concept provides a particularly effective structure for the resolution of conflict (see Chapter 3).

There are also significant differences in training methodology. Participants are asked to bring real tasks from their actual work, and these are used as vehicles for learning in group and individual working sessions. (An incidental benefit from this approach is that participants probably make some progress in these tasks, which reduces the 'opportunity cost' referred to earlier.) I believe that working on real tasks increases the relevance of learning. If artificial tasks are used, it tends to leave unanswered the question, 'How does this relate to the real work, if at all?'

Group sessions are all videorecorded and analysis is conducted using the tape – a review is literally a 're-view'. Used in this way, video is an enormously powerful learning tool. It enables people to see themselves as others see them, and the experience is always a surprise if not a shock. They see how easily their well-meant actions can have the opposite effect to that intended. At the same time they are offered alternative techniques which they can try out in subsequent sessions. Video makes it possible to carry out a microscopic examination of incidents, going back over them as often as is necessary in order to understand what actually happened.

Video is such a powerful medium for learning that its use requires special skill and discretion on the part of a trainer. It is all too tempting for him to focus on what goes wrong as the area for improvement, without putting it in the context of all that goes well and the positive intent behind unsuccessful efforts. The videotape can be left to speak for itself; course members are far more critical of themselves than a trainer is ever likely to be. It is his job to make sure they balance their self-appraisal by appreciating their achievements as well as their shortcomings.

Because at Synectics we train internal company trainers to carry out the Innovative Teamwork Programme, we have spelled out in some detail the role of a Synectics trainer, as follows:

The function of a Synectics trainer is to facilitate the learning of course members. He/she does so by:

1. Creating an environment conducive to learning – relaxed, non-threatening, encouraging of risktaking, positive;
2. Modelling in his/her own behaviour the Synectics principles – good listening, clarity about his/her action responsibility and respect for the action responsibility of others, open-mindedness, responsiveness to the needs and wishes of others, good teamworker;
3. Providing feedback which is constructive, positive, and 'timely' in that it connects with the current learning needs of course members;
4. Providing input from the Synectics body of knowledge, and his/her experience of using it, as and when he/she judges it will contribute to course members' learning – and not otherwise!
5. Designing and setting up learning experiments to provide a sequence of learning steps that are easily understood and absorbed (these are largely provided in the course design, but the trainer has some discretion in deciding the exact sequence, pace, selection of exercises, etc.).

This description of the trainer's role has implications for the way a trainer operates. First and foremost, he is not a teacher in the conventional sense of the expert 'jug' pouring out its knowledge of a subject into empty 'mugs'. (Many course members come with the unconscious assumption that this *is* the trainer's role, having as their model their own school and university experiences).

To correct this assumption, a trainer must behave at all times in ways which respect the autonomy and self-respect of course members. They are experienced and successful managers who already know a lot, from their own experience, about the subject matter of the course (human behaviour at work). They must be treated as equals and never put in a 'one-down' position on account of their trainer's superior knowledge of his speciality. A trainer's role is that of a specialist coach, or a master in the true sense – one who set out on the road before the pupil did, and has therefore travelled further along it than the pupil.

Secondly, a trainer must model in his own behaviour those kinds of behaviour he recommends – particularly by:

— recognizing what is his own action responsibility (items 1–5 above) and what is the action responsibility of course members (their own learning);
— listening attentively to course members, and paraphrasing his understanding of what they are saying;
— accepting the opinions of course members as truths about them and valid for them (he doesn't have to agree);
— assuming constructive intent as regards course members' behaviour (both in sessions and in discussions).

It's what you *do*, not what you *say*, as a trainer that has the greatest impact.

It is, of course, quite contrary to Synectics principles to ask questions without saying why you are asking. This immediately rules out the use of questions in the way that teachers often use them, either to test knowledge or to elicit a point that they want to make. If you already know the answer, do not ask the question. Doing so puts course members in the position of having to 'guess what you have in mind', a potentially 'one-down' position.

Equally, do not get into arguments of the 'I'm right, you're wrong' variety, which are potentially punishing: accept a person's view as valid for him, and if you have a different view, say so, as a truth about yourself.

Participants on a Synectics course learn primarily from their experience of the things they do (the sessions and exercises), secondly from the video feedback, thirdly from their colleagues, and *lastly* from their trainer. A trainer's role is a relatively humble one: to set up learning experiments and allow the learning process to take place. It follows that it is not necessary to do a lot of talking; in fact the less talking a trainer indulges in, the better a course turns out. I suspect that most of us talk too much; it's a great temptation when you are enthusiastic and knowledgeable about a subject, but it inhibits learning!

There is one other, rather comforting, implication of this view of a Synectics trainer's role: you do not have to be perfect! You do not have to know the answers to all the questions course members may put to you. It's quite adequate to say, 'I don't know', 'I've never thought of it in that way', 'That's an interesting new angle', 'I'll check with my colleagues to see if they know', etc. By doing so, as well as taking the pressure off yourself, you model for course attenders the key quality of being open to learning. If you are perfect, you cannot have anything to learn! It is possible, and necessary, to combine being professional, competent, prepared and confident, with being human, fallible, liable to make mistakes and willing to learn from them!

Adventure Training

This generic label covers a wide variety of Outward Bound type courses which have in common the use of outdoor activities as the medium of development of both individual and team skills. The underlying assumption is that by engaging in very different activities from those normally undertaken at work, participants become aware of the personal and internal processes involved in the completing of the exercises set.

Terry Simons, an independent consultant who has been engaged in this field for most of the post-war period, puts this type of training into an historical perspective:

Coming as it did, in the 1950s, many potential buyers were ex-service senior officers who were looking for a civilian replacement for military methods.

The problem was that organization theories which specified job descriptions in terms of reporting relationships said very little about the human being who filled a particular role. At the same time there was a reaction against institutionalism on the part of the smarter potential young executive.

So the old warriors took on ex-service trainers to devise ways to legitimize forced marches and physical deprivation because 'it never did me any harm'. These trainers looked for help not only from the biographies of great leaders but also from the emerging behavioural sciences. Simple formulae began to appear.

The new formulae seemed not to work without the physical hardship, and ways of turning this hardship into 'skills training' began to appear. Managers were persuaded of the necessity to tie figure-of-eight knots, to ford rivers, and to stay awake for long periods.

With the admission of T-group training into the rules of the game it became okay to replace much of the received theory with mutual 'feedback'. At the end of the physical torment it was said that honest discussion would become even more honest because it was based on mutual experience, even though participants may have had to travel hundreds of miles from their mutual workplace to do it.

Out of all the experiments in the alchemy of leadership a few emerged as successful long-term programmes. Some religion-based programmes were offering independent views and opportunities for meditation and counselling These still exist, but serve quietly and are only found by recommendation. Others found a simple formula that a growing organization could use as a ready-made common culture. The latter would print their gospel on plastic reminder cards that, while still gathering dust in corners of offices, remind the manager of good intentions.

Good leaders emerged from the programmes, and sometimes did lay the credit at their doors. But the courses provided a more important service to the training/development manager who hired them.

All of these programmes were part of a wider programme in the company. Although occasionally there would be a single representative from a company, mostly there was a planned campaign. By having the keys to an external experience that not only was personally beneficial as a physical holiday but also was a necessary rite of passage into the 'in' group in the company, the nominating manager had great power. Sometimes the company changed its politics, and usually if the training manager went, his 'leadership' course went with him, and some new magic replaced it. This, more than anything else, demonstrated the shibboleth nature of the training.

Personal feedback, disinterested opinions, having to get things done outside one's familiar territory, all might have an effect on leadership potential. Most of all, they tend to separate the leader from the follower, and to show the follower how to respect and follow leadership. True originality and creative leadership usually play mayhem with leadership courses.

To varying degrees in different programmes, there is provision for explicit review and learning after each exercise, the quality of which depends heavily on the skill of tutors. The Leadership Trust stresses to its tutors that 'the real learning takes place in the appraisals and reviews. It is essential to dig deep and identify underlying factors, strengths (and how to exploit them) and weaknesses (and how to cope with them). There are several opportunities for the participants to appraise and this is where self-awareness leading to self-realization really starts.'

There is no doubt that programmes of this kind are highly popular with the majority of participants – and hated by others. They seem to generate extreme reactions – love or hate. My own experience is limited to a long weekend (it seemed *very* long) and a single day, so I do not claim to be an authority on the subject.

There was certainly for me exhilaration in discovering in my mid-fifties that I was able to learn to rock-climb and abseil down a rock-face (albeit in very safe conditions set up by expert tutors). Equally, I was not amused by being put in the situation of having to build a raft from barrels, planks and rope at four o'clock in the morning in order to cross an estuary and finish acting out a complicated scenario devised by the course designer.

Some of the general influences noted earlier – the bonding effect of shared strange experiences, the potential for learning from any experience, the whole Hawthorn effect of focusing attention on teamwork issues – work in favour of this kind of programme. Certainly the strangeness of the experiences, the contrast of physical outdoor activities with the normal sedentary cerebral routines of managers in business, can have a mind-stretching and unblocking effect which opens the participant's mind to learning.

But I still have reservations about the whole cult of Adventure Training. I am suspicious of its armed services origins and its association with the authoritarian traditions of the military. There is a strong flavour of the Boy Scouts, and part of the enthusiasm of participants seems to come from reliving happy scouting days (and nights) of their youth (not that I see any harm in that!).

More seriously, I doubt the *relevance* of these activities to the work of managers, especially senior managers and others working in an innovative environment. (They may be more appropriate for managers in a high pressure operational environment, with complex choices to be made under time constraints. With increasing automation, planning and computer control, the number of environments of this kind is likely to diminish substantially.)

Essentially, the tasks involved are what Professor Revans calls puzzles as opposed to problems – a puzzle involves discovering an already known solution, a problem requires the development of a solution where none exists. By definition the process of innovation deals with problems, not puzzles. The senior management of businesses of any size ought to be busy creating the future of the company, leaving day-to-day operations to lower levels of management.

If we return to the Critchley Casey model (described in Chapter 2), we see that it is *only* when dealing with true *problems* that a high level of teamwork is actually needed. To practise teamwork on puzzles, where simple co-operative skills are all that is required, seems superfluous.

Thus, 'to get both barrels and the fluid in them, all your team and yourself past the finishing line in forty minutes, without any person, equipment or barrels touching the ground' is clearly a puzzle with a solution known to the trainer, and calling for expertise in the use of ropes, pulleys, planks, scaffolding and other equipment provided. How it relates to the work of a manager in business (assuming he is not running a construction site!) escapes me, though I have no doubt connections could be made.

Similarly, on the overnight exercise I found myself trapped in, one of the teams came up with a simple and elegant solution to one of the 'problems' posed. It was immediately ruled out of order by the course tutor because it did not fit in with the planned course of the exercise – which immediately lost much of its point as far as I was concerned.

Perhaps the greatest single objection to the use of puzzles in this way is the effect it produces on the relationship between the course tutor and participants. It puts the tutor in the position of saying, 'I know something you don't know, and you have to find it out', leaving the participants feeling 'one down' and 'set up' – not a good state of mind for learning. (It was for this reason that my company discontinued the use of a sort of puzzle at the beginning of its courses, even though it was open to alternative solutions.)

However, rather than leave you with my own rather jaundiced view of the subject, I will give the last word to Terry Simons, who has been a tutor on a number of these programmes:

Some of the activities retain a military flavour – climbing, diving and foot-slogging; getting wet is normal. These are a small part of the learning experience. Most of the tasks are highly stylized problems with a given kit – poles, planks, ropes, and yet more water. These problems punctuate a continuous tutor-led group development that is unique to each team.

A large number of courses are designed around a facility. A new hotel decides that it will attract a regular clientele by working with a training team. This team is usually part of the outdoors sub-culture of climbers/canoers/mountain leaders who just want a living in the open air. The legitimization can be done by process consultants who would be just as effective anywhere.

Adventure centres that were originally built for children have found that the scale of charges that they can make to industry gives them a better return, and most of them offer some sort of course.

Longer business school courses have now realized that they are looked upon by active young executives with greater favour if they can offer a couple of weeks in the middle at a more romantic place, and some of them have combined with the PE departments to put something on.

In summary, they all tend to be 'followership' courses with a measure of self-revelation on influencing skills and guts. They tend to be an extension of company culture, to be used as rites of passage for intending managers. They pretend a magic to be got at the peak, so long a you get there the hard way, and that submission to the gorilla in gym shoes compliantly will transform you into 'officers and gentlemen'.

Psychological approaches

From the T-groups of the sixties, through the Gestalt Therapy and Transactional Analysis of the seventies, to today's Neuro-linguistic Programming, there have been a host of psychological/psycho-therapeutic approaches which have been applied to a greater or lesser extent to the improvement of teamwork in the business environment. I have experimented, cautiously, with a few of them, and I take a guarded and restricted view of their suitability or desirability in this field.

There seem to be two assumptions behind this type of training. The first is that if people have a better understanding of the psychological factors at work in group processes, they are able to handle them better. To the extent that they have a common language in which to talk about them, I agree with this proposition, simply because I believe it is more constructive to talk about interpersonal problems than to act them out.

I have to admit I observe a paradox here: the people who are most knowledgeable in these matters seem to be the ones who cause the most emotional problems in a team, while the cheerful, uncomplicated ones who are a pleasure to work with often know very little about psychological theories! (Perhaps it's like physical health: the naturally healthy are not very interested in diseases!)

The second assumption is altogether more questionable. It is that if team members experience some kind of group therapy, they emerge a better team, more understanding and more trusting. They may indeed, but this depends a great deal on the skill of the therapist and the existing level of trust in the team. A team that works reasonably well together may in fact shift to a higher level of trust under the guidance of a skilled therapist. But most of the teams I observe greatly improve their performance by much simpler and less risky steps, of the kind described in this book, before venturing into such deep waters.

I am also concerned about the possible invasion of personal privacy. Group therapy can open up some highly personal aspects of an individual's life which he may have no wish to share with his working colleagues. Certainly no team member should be forced to go into such a session, either directly or by peer group pressure; and if one team member declines, for the rest of the team to go ahead would be divisive.

The practice of psychotherapy is far from being an exact science, and therapies come and go with a frequency that is rather alarming. Richard Bandler, the guru of Neuro-linguistic Programming (the current vogue), has some scathing comments to make about both Transactional Analysis and Gestalt Therapy. Of TA he writes, 'Not everybody in the world has a parent, adult and child that argue with each other. You won't find much of that in Tahiti. You have to go to a therapist to learn to have those problems.' And of Gestalt Therapy, 'People learn repeated *sequences* of behaviour, and not necessarily the content. The sequence you learn in Gestalt Therapy is the following: When you feel sad or frustrated, you hallucinate old friends and relatives, become angry and violent, and then you feel better and other people are nice to you. Take that sequence into the real world without the content . . . How's that for a model of human relationships.'*

I cannot wait to read what the authors of the *next* breakthrough in psychotherapy have to say about Neuro-linguistic Programming!

Team and management conferences

Increasingly, business organizations are feeling the need to get the entire management team together for a couple of days each year for a company conference. I believe the instinct is soundly based; it is potentially extremely valuable for a whole team to reaffirm its purpose, clarify the direction in which it is going, and create and renew links between those of its parts that do not frequently come into contact with each other. A good conference can send its delegates away with batteries recharged, confidence renewed and enthusiasm rekindled.

But results like these do not automatically flow from simply having a conference. Quite apart from the cost of a conference (both

*Richard Bandler, *Using Your Brain – for a Change*, Real People Press, 1985.

in terms of financial expenses and the diversion of management time from current operations), a poorly run conference can do more harm than good. It can strengthen cynicism and spread dissatisfaction through an organization; the management of a conference reflects the management of a business as a whole.

To structure the proceedings to ensure that fifty or one hundred participants have a worthwhile and rewarding experience is a complex task. Often it is tacitly avoided; the formal proceedings are treated as mere ceremony, benefit actually accruing from informal contact in the bars, over meals, and so on.

Such an attitude represents, in my view, an abdication of responsiblity. The formal aspect of a conference provides a major opportunity to achieve worthwhile results, informal contact being enriched by high quality formal sessions.

The key to a successful conference is active and meaningful participation by all its delegates throughout the greater part of the proceedings. This cannot be brought about by a simple series of presentations, however skilfully they are given and even if they are followed by questions and discussion. The amount of 'air time' available to the individual delegate is minimal; he is asked to spend 99 per cent of the time listening. Listening effectively is hard work, and I believe it is unrealistic to expect conference delegates to maintain attention over long periods without active participation. (I know that political parties run their annual conferences in this way, which is almost a good enough reason in itself for *not* doing the same!)

The simplest way to provide for participation is to split a conference up into working groups or syndicates (preferably not exceeding eight persons per syndicate, because this seems empirically to be the maximum number for an effective participative meeting). Syndicate-working of itself, however, does not guarantee that discussions are meaningful and rewarding. It is not enough to say, 'Break up into groups, discuss the presentation you have just heard and report back to the plenary session in forty-five minutes.' Participants need to know why they are discussing it, what they are expected to achieve, and what will be done with their output. (Too often managements seem to expect syndicates to regurgitate the presentation, and syndicates set out to tell top management what they think top management want to hear!)

Syndicate sessions provide a good opportunity to find out what participants really think and feel about a business, and to collect their ideas on how that business can be moved forward – assuming top management wants to know these things! To get these results sessions need to be correctly structured and run by somebody with at least a modest understanding of how to conduct such a meeting. My own preference is to appoint facilitators/moderators to run syndicate sessions, giving them some training in how to do this before the conference.

One of their duties is to record the ideas generated and conclusions reached by groups. Usually these are reported back to the full conference. Alternatively, information sheets can be pinned up round the conference room, and everybody given the chance to wander round and study the output of all the groups. This creates an interesting 'street market' atmosphere and is a refreshing change from sitting in serried ranks in the conference hall.

The output of the groups needs to be taken seriously, and be *seen* to be taken seriously, by top management. It is worth the effort to get the sheets typed and circulated as a conference record. Along with this report, there needs to be a statement from the top team of the initiatives it intends to take as a result of the conference output. It may well decide to set up some task groups or working parties to pursue further some of the issues raised. These post-conference activities provide a natural link to the following year's conference, which can begin with a review of what has been achieved since the previous one.

One of the most difficult tasks of a conference designer is to vary the design over the years so that it does not become stereotyped. One of my clients, for example, decided after two years of successful conferences on the lines described above, that they wanted something different – less business related, more light-hearted, but still a worthwhile use of time. They opted to run a management game on personal computers in syndicate teams; it worked extremely well, providing a high level of involvement, new experiences and potential learning about teamwork.

The social aspects of a conference are also worth giving some thought to. It may be that unstructured informal contacts are all that is needed, but a conscious decision should be taken that this is the case – it should not be assumed. There is a risk that people will only talk to those they know already and miss the opportunity to make new contacts.

The alternative is to put some structure into the social events. I have on occasion set groups to work on such tasks as writing and performing a company song, with impressive results in terms of the energy, wit and creativity that is revealed. Other forms of internal cabaret have a similar effect. On the other hand you can call in professionals to stage-manage a murder mystery (preferably with the chief executive as victim.)

It is a matter of judgement whether or not these kinds of activity are appropriate to a particular organization at a particular time. (It would be highly insensitive to organize a cabaret just after a wave of redundancies, for example!) I am sure that an enjoyable and memorable experience is good for a team, but I know no way of guaranteeing that an experience is viewed in this way by everyone. There is usually somebody who objects to being involved in what they see as 'silly games', and if that is a widely held view, it is probably better not to push them.

7. Assessing the teamwork

How do you know how well your team is doing? Is there any way, however qualitative, in which it is possible to measure something as intangible as teamwork?

However difficult it may be, people do make judgements of this kind, both about teams they belong to and teams with which they interact. And professionals in this field (myself included) cheerfully pontificate on the subject to anyone who will pay them to do so. It is, in fact, necessary to make such judgements (explicitly or implicitly) if there is to be a basis on which to decide how to go about improving the quality of teamwork in a given situation.

In this chapter I present the factors that I take into account, and suggest ways of going about making a judgement.

Task performance

Improving teamwork is not (for a business, at least) an end in itself (it could be for a religious community or a boy scout troop). It is a means of achieving higher performance in those tasks that a team exists to carry out. Since performance in most cases is relatively easy to measure, it may seem that we have a simple answer to our question: a team that is working well is a successful team, and vice versa.

I believe this is broadly true, with a couple of important

qualifications. The first concerns the criteria according to which performance is judged; they may be set misleadingly low or misleadingly high. A low-performing team which is allowed to set its own objectives sets them at a level it feels can be achieved comfortably, way below its potential. Likewise, a team that is working well may have objectives set for it (or even set them itself) which are so far out of reach as to be meaningless as a measure of performance. It is important, therefore, to look critically at objectives and the way they are set, before using performance data to judge how well a team is working.

Environmental factors also need to be taken into account. It is easy to look like a team of heroes, for a year or two, if you happen to be in a market that is expanding rapidly (like that of home computers in the recent past). How you perform in the period subsequent to the boom is the real test of your teamwork. Equally, developments like the Falklands War or the year-long coal strike can blow the best teams off course if they happen to be directly affected.

There can also be a significant time-lag in a business environment between completion of an activity and its results. Companies can continue to prosper for years on the advantages gained by initiatives made in the distant past, almost without regard to the quality of current work. (When I worked for Rank Xerox in the late sixties, the technical and commercial leadership established in earlier years almost guaranteed continued growth and rising profits independently of the current activities of the people in the business!). In reversing a decline, many years of good work may have to be put in before an improvement begins to show in the performance figures. Similarly in a new enterprise, some years tilling the soil and sowing will probably be needed before the harvest becomes visible.

Ask the team

Part of a team leader's job is to keep his finger on the pulse of his team's (and individual team members') morale and motivation. He does this by talking to team members singly and in groups – and particularly by listening to them sensitively. Formal review sessions, such as the feedback and appraisal sessions described in Chapter 3, provide one means of collecting data, the informal day-to-day contact of normal operations another.

Team meetings can (and should) be used to pose the question,

'How well are we doing as a team?' Information is best collected in the form of a group 'itemized response', in which team members are asked to identify all the aspects of the team working they are pleased with, and those they wish to change. Each individual's view is accepted as true for him, without argument as to whether it is right or wrong, justified or unjustified. The aspects members wish to change are then the subject of group problem-solving, to find generally acceptable ways of making desired changes without losing the good features.

Unfortunately, these direct methods only work successfully when the team climate is such that members feel able to express their views openly and honestly and say what they really mean. A team that is not working well talks in coded generalizations that mean very little and provide no specific starting point for problem-solving. If a team is in a really bad way, members remain silent rather than say what they think.

Attitude surveys conducted by questionnaire provide a way of collecting data anonymously. They can also be repeated on a regular basis in order to measure changes in the state of a team. In my view, they are an essential feature of any long-term programme of change. They are most commonly carried out on complete organizations rather than individual teams, though there is no reason why they should not be carried out on individual teams, if there is felt to be a need to collect information in this way.

As with any questionnaire-based technique, there is always a risk that questions may be misunderstood or that answers may not be given honestly. You do not need to devise your own questionnaire from scratch; you can start with a tested questionnaire (e.g. the one provided in *Beat the System!* by Robert F. Allen*) and adapt the wording to your own precise needs.

If you decide to use an attitude survey, you have to be prepared to publish the results and act on them. There can be a backlash if the expectations raised by conducting it are not met by subsequent action. People feel disgruntled: 'They asked for our opinions and then ignored them.'

There is also a danger that managements react against findings when they turn out to be unpalatable. They claim either that the survey is in some way inaccurate or misleading, or that the respondents 'don't understand' what the management is doing. That gap in understanding is precisely what a survey is intended to reveal, highlighting the need for better communication on the part of management.

*McGraw Hill, 1980.

For a quick snapshot of how a team's members view the quality of their teamwork, you can ask each of them to write down a score, in strictest confidence, on a scale of 1 to 10, which you then collect. You can publish the result as an average (mean, mode, median, or preferably all three), or more meaningfully as a complete listing, without names. The danger of the complete list is that it may highlight one or two malcontents. Their discontent needs to be known about by the leader, but it may be preferable to deal with them privately rather than in a full team meeting.

Ask an outsider

There are a lot of consultants (myself included) who happily talk to team members individually and report their findings without identifying individual contributions. (This approach is similar to depth interviewing in qualitative market research.) A consultant may also conduct group discussions with or without the team leader present.

The value of this approach rests heavily on the skill of the consultant, particularly as an interviewer. He needs to establish quickly an environment which encourages a respondent to open up and speak freely. Having done so, he needs to be a superb listener, picking up what is *not* being said, as well as what is, and to be attentive to nuances of tone and non-verbal signals – at the same time capturing the essence in his notes, or recording the conversation on tape if a respondent agrees. He must probe for more depth without interposing his own views or asking loaded questions.

Having amassed all this data, he has to make sense of it. If he is lucky, it falls naturally into a manageable pattern. The great danger is that he imposes on the data his own preconceptions, and the more experienced he is the more likely he is to have them! The experience that makes him a skilled and perceptive interviewer can lead him into hearing what he expects to hear!

Other outsiders interact with a team in the normal course of its operation, particularly its 'customers' – i.e. the recipients of its output – and specialists such as staff of the company's personnel department. Their impressions are worth canvassing, discreetly, since they are formed as by-products of everyday transactions rather than a special enquiry, and will not be contaminated by the enquiry itself.

Characteristics of a good team

Many years ago I was travelling with a colleague much older than myself. We were to stay at an unknown provincial hotel. As we approached it, but still at a distance of two hundred yards, he said, 'My god, I can smell it already', and went on to describe graphically the odour of stale food, damp and cigarette smoke that would assail our nostrils the moment we stepped inside. He was absolutely right – years of travelling in the UK had taught him the warning signs.

I have a similar way of anticipating the quality of teamwork in the many different organizations I work with. I believe I can 'smell' it almost as I walk through the door. I have tried to identify below the characteristics which seem to me to be indicators of good teamwork:

— People smile, genuinely and naturally.
— There is plenty of laughter – genuine belly-laughs as opposed to nervous, embarrassed laughter.
— People are confident, a 'can do' rather than 'can't do' group.
— They are loyal to their team and to each other – they do not denigrate colleagues or the organization.
— They are relaxed and friendly, not tense and hostile.
— They are open to outsiders and interested in the world about them.
— They are energetic, lively and active.
— They are enterprising, taking the initiative rather than reacting to events.
— They listen to and do not interrupt each other (or me!).

This is a highly personal list: you may like to draw up your own. And then score your own team against it.

Conclusion

On re-reading my manuscript and reaching this point, I felt the need for some concluding remarks to tie it all together. It was then that my colleague, Terry Cooke-Davies, handed me a paper he had just written about project management and project teams.

'I wish I had written that,' I said, as soon as I had read it; 'It's just what I need to conclude my teamwork book.'

'Use it anyway you want,' replied Terry, and after some hesitation, I decided to do just that.

Before I quote him, however, I would like to reflect on the teamwork implications of the incident. To get (and to give) the help that is needed precisely *when* it is required is the essence of good teamwork. So why did I hesitate before taking up the offer?

I think it was because of a feeling that this occasion was too one-sided – there was no *quid pro quo*. Then I realized that in the give and take of teamwork there are times to take as well as times to give. In a supportive environment, you have to be prepared to be supported as well as to support.

So, with thanks to Terry and also to another colleague, Barre Fitzpatrick, whose ideas are quoted by Terry, here are some concluding words about teamwork.

'The key to success is deceptively simple, and surprisingly obvious. In a word, it is energy. Energy, both individual and collective, both human and natural, is 'the difference that makes the difference'.

In a team which consistently wins, it seems as if each individual performs to the peak of his or her own performance, and the team as a whole achieves a greatness which is more than the sum of the individuals. It is as if the team has a life of its own, and by 'tuning in' to this 'being', each individual can raise his own game for the good of the team. You could almost say that the energies of each member of the team somehow match, complement and augment each other, to produce a team energy which is greater than the sum of the individuals'.

The team manager, therefore, can see his role as focussing the energy of individuals and separate groups towards winning the game, even though they are scattered and separated.

It was a Synectics colleague of mine, Barre Fitzpatrick, who first drew to my attention the behaviour of a strange organism, or rather an accumulation of organisms, called cellular slime mould (*Dictyostelium discoideum*), and just how much it resembled the performance of teams.

Dicky, as I shall call this rather endearing being, lies in a kind of evolutionary no man's land, somewhere between the single-celled amoeba and the true multi-cellular organism.

Most of the time, the separate amoebae of which Dicky is made up roam around old bits of wood and dead leaves, looking for their favourite kind of bacteria to feed on and every now and then multiplying like all other amoebae. If food begins to run a bit short, however, the separate amoebae begin to cluster into small groups of perhaps a few dozen individuals. These clusters then congregate into a single blob, called a 'grex', which might contain thousands of amoebae.

Having got himself together, as it were, some of Dicky's cells begin to climb up over the backs of their colleagues, until they form first a hemispherical dome, and then a cone with a nipple on top. At this point, Dicky topples over onto his side, and becomes a small 'slug', able to move across the forest floor in the direction of light. The nipple is raised and leads the way.

When Dicky finds another source of food, he is likely to dissolve again into thousands of individual amoebae, each going their separate way.

Barre, who is Irish and a scholar of philosophy and psychology, had been describing how he kept the energy constructive in a problem-solving group by recognizing certain patterns of interaction as likely to lead to problems. It seems that one way of looking at the leader's job is to regard him as there to direct the group's energy towards harmony and achieving group goals. In this respect, he is performing a similar function to the conductor of an orchestra, bringing out the best in each of the players, but also keeping an eye on the score.

If this is right, then the role of a process leader in projects becomes critical at those times when Dicky has got himself together and needs to go off looking for another source of food.*

If the process leader does his unobtrusive job well, then Dicky manages the transition from cluster of amoebae to mobile organism smoothly, and finds nourishment somewhere else. Then it becomes safe for the individuals to go off on their separate ways again, finding new food supplies for themselves, thanks to the performance of the group as a whole.

On the other hand, for most of Dicky's life he is either a widely scattered colony of individual amoebae, or a series of small clusters.

This is where the team leader/project manager comes in. He or she is that invisible sensory organ by which the being that is Dicky keeps in touch with the separate constituent parts. It is the project manager's job to be sensitive to the needs and energy of all the individual amoebae and small clusters, so that groups can begin to form when the food supply begins to run short. How he does this is unique to each individual, but some of the elements which are common to all high-performing managers are now becoming clear.

The first is a range of highly developed communication skills. This is not surprising, in view of the separateness of the different elements of the team. The range of skills, however, includes not only the obvious, such as listening, speaking, and writing, but some much less common ones such as the ability to communicate complex concpts using image, metaphor and analogy. In this wider sense, it seems to me that communication is a whole body activity, not just a function of the ears, eyes and mouth. One very important aspect is the ability to 'tune in' to the messages which are being transmitted to you (and by you) outside your normal level of awareness.

In every day language, this kind of whole body communication is often labelled 'intuition'. People will tell you that they 'sense something is wrong' with what they are being told, even if they 'can't quite put their finger' on what it is. The most successful project managers I have ever met have all told me how much they rely on their intuition. In a similar vein, when I ask groups of experienced project managers to think back to projects which have gone wrong, they invariably identify some point in the project at which they 'sensed something was wrong', long before the wheel actually came off and the project crashed.

*i.e. at times of innovation.

The project manager, then, sets up and maintains communication channels between the individuals and clusters who are working alone, and the being which is more than the individuals – in essence, Dicky himself. To do this, there are all kinds of tools which he can use, but these are of no use unless he can tune in both to Dicky's wavelength and to the wavelengths of the individuals in their separate states. These communication channels are essentially two-way, so that the team is aware of each individual and each individual is aware of the team.

When there is evidence that the team and an individual, or several individuals, are drifting apart, or even worse directing some of their energy against other members of the team, then the project manager needs to call the team together again. This is when his skill as a process leader will once again evoke the sense of group identity, and raise the level of the team's performance.

You can see what effect this can have on the project by looking at a kind of 'energy curve' representing the amount of energy, enthusiasm, or optimism exuded by the team throughout the project's life. After the initial enthusiasm and optimism, there is a kind of 'honeymoon period' which can last any time from a few hours to a few months. During this period, the team members seem to be bolstered by their common vision of the benefits which the project will bring.

The next phase is often a kind of progressive awareness that things aren't going to be as easy as was hoped. The team energy seems to drop off during this phase, sometimes relatively slowly (if the team is closeknit and members are on each other's wavelengths), and sometimes relatively quickly (if the energy turns inwards against members of the team). In the second case, certain characteristic phrases begin to be heard: 'Why weren't we told?', 'Who allowed that?', 'Don't look at me, that's not my responsibility.', and in the most dangerous instances, 'What are we doing this for, anyway?'. Perhaps one rule of thumb for the project manager who notices phrases like this becoming commonplace is 'Get the team together, and fast!'.

But whether the decline in energy is slow or fast, there seems to come a time when the original food supply is insufficient to sustain the team's life. This is a time of crisis for both the team and its leader. What is needed is a new source of energy for the team as a whole, and we have already talked about how a skilful project manager can help the team to provide that. In a long project lasting for months or even years, this cycle is likely to repeat itself many times, with the project-workers feeding separately in one area until the nourishment becomes scarce, then congregating and moving to a new level of team awareness before re-separating.

It isn't too much of an exaggeration to term this period the 'zone of crisis' for the project, since at any time, if the energy falls below a certain critical level, the project will die.

In addition to monitoring the energy curve of the project, another valuable indicator of the health of the project team is what the energy is being focussed on. One useful model in this context is the triple circle of task, group and individual. We have already seen that in teams which persistently win, the amount of group energy seems to be very high, so that the team focusses very effectively on the task.

If we look at the opposite situation for a moment, in a team which is losing, there is often very little energy available for either task or group needs. On the contrary, the available energy seems to be directed towards sustaining and even protecting the individual. In many companies this same focus is widely recognized as 'cover your arse' behaviour, with all its trimmings – the oft repeated 'Don't blame me for this mess.' and memos sent by anyone who feels that the 'shit-coloured spotlight' might be turned on them next.

Each of these three different kinds of energy, if it becomes the primary focus of an individual member of the team, will make itself felt in its own characteristic way. A member of a project team performing a specific task will behave rather differently, and communicate his or her progress in ways which are subtly different, according to whether he or she is doing the job in order to get results (task focus), make a helpful contribution to the team as a whole (group focus), or serve his or her own interests in some way (individual focus). Paradoxically, in a high-performance team, it seems as if all three areas complement each other effortlessly.

So it rather looks as if a team which wants to win can learn something from Dicky. If the team as a whole can stay healthy, vigorous and full of life, there will be plenty of energy available for the task of winning. In a healthy body, each cell contributes to the overall quality of life, while being fulfilled in its own specialist function. An effective project manager monitors the health of each cell, while a skilful process leader takes the body to places where there is sufficient nourishment for the whole being.